LIVERPOOL FC
On This Day

LIVERPOOL FC
On This Day

*History, Facts & Figures
from Every Day of the Year*

DAVID CLAYTON

LIVERPOOL FC
On This Day
History, Facts & Figures from Every Day of the Year

All statistics, facts and figures are correct as of 31st August 2011

© David Clayton

David Clayton has asserted his rights in accordance with the Copyright, Designs and Patents Act 1988 to be identified as the author of this work.

Published By:
Pitch Publishing (Brighton) Ltd
A2 Yeoman Gate
Yeoman Way
Durrington
BN13 3QZ

Email: info@pitchpublishing.co.uk
Web: www.pitchpublishing.co.uk

First published 2011
Reprinted 2012, 2014, 2015, 2017, 2018, 2019

A catalogue record for this book is available from the British Library

ISBN 978-1-9080510-5-9

Typesetting and origination by Pitch Publishing
Printed and bound in India by Replika Press

For Samantha and Scotty

ACKNOWLEDGEMENTS

Thanks to Dan Tester, my long-suffering editor for patience above and beyond the call of duty. Thanks to Alex Rowen and Will Unwin and especially Paul at Pitch Publishing for not hiring a team of hitmen to pay me a visit after numerous deadlines sailed past. Thanks to my family – Sarah my wife and my beautiful children Harry, Jaime and Chrissie.

INTRODUCTION

Liverpool Football Club – renowned and loved around the world (outside Manchester and the confines of Goodison Park) and more of an institution than a team. What makes Liverpool so special?

Why do people from every background around the globe make this Merseyside giant one of the best-supported teams on the planet?

To find the answers to the above, you need look no further than *Liverpool On This Day* and track the Reds' journey from a side that were moderately successful with a decent fan-base, who suddenly moved up into a different stratosphere.

Though the team that were spawned from an Anfield divorce with Everton enjoyed success before World War II, they were drifting somewhat after the hostilities ended, particularly during the 1950s when the club hit an all-time low.

Clearly, none of the above put Liverpool on the world map of football, but remarkably, one man did. Bill Shankly's passion for the club seeped into every blade of grass on the Anfield pitch and his desire transferred into the hearts and minds of every player who played for him and all the Liverpool fans.

He was Liverpool Football Club and, in so many ways, he still is. His beliefs that football was a simple game, built around very basic instructions of passing the ball, and moving and working together as a team, in every aspect.

Liverpool On This Day has events, results, transfers, births and deaths that have occurred throughout the Reds' history. There is at least one entry for every day of the year dating back to the club's formation right through to the re-signing of Craig Bellamy in August 2011.

There's something for everyone and it's a book you can dip in and out of on any given day of the year; open, read and see what was happening on that day in the past.

David Clayton

LIVERPOOL FC
On This Day

JANUARY

MONDAY 1st JANUARY 1934

An awful start to the New Year as Liverpool are thrashed 9-2 away to Newcastle United. First-half goals from Harold Taylor and an own goal from Alec Betton, can't stop the Reds shipping a hatful of goals after the break and as a result, George Patterson's side slip to 18th, just five points off the foot of Division One.

SATURDAY 1st JANUARY 1966

Liverpool make the perfect start to the New Year with a 2-1 win over Manchester United at Anfield. Tommy Smith scores the Reds' first and Gordon Milne grabs an 88th-minute winner to send the 53,970 fans wild.

MONDAY 1st JANUARY 2007

Three goals in 22 second-half minutes give Liverpool a welcome 3-0 Premier League win over Sam Allardyce's third-place Bolton Wanderers. The victory sees the Reds leapfrog Wanderers into third and the goals are scored by Peter Crouch (61), Steven Gerrard (63) and Dirk Kuyt on 83 minutes.

SATURDAY 1st JANUARY 2011

Chasing a first win at Anfield since 1954, Bolton Wanderers take a 1-0 lead when Kevin Davies fires the Trotters ahead just before half-time to pile more misery on Roy Hodgson and his troubled reign as Liverpool boss. With just over 35,000 attending a Bank Holiday fixture – the Reds' lowest crowd for seven years – it is clear the fans have had enough of the former Fulham boss, but a Fernando Torres equaliser on 49 minutes and a Joe Cole winner two minutes into added time give the hosts a 2-1 win – but Hodgson's days are clearly numbered.

SATURDAY 2nd JANUARY 1965

The Reds come back from the dead in a thrilling match away to Blackpool. Having already drawn 2-2 at Anfield earlier in the season, the Seasiders again prove tough opposition and take a 2-0 lead into the half-time break. However, two Roger Hunt goals on 53 and 58 minutes, and a 75th-minute winner from Ian St John, turn the game on its head to give Liverpool a thrilling 3-2 win. A crowd of almost 22,000 pack Bloomfield Road for the five-goal feast.

SATURDAY 2nd JANUARY 1971

James McLaughlin's 28th-minute goal gives the Reds a narrow 1-0 victory over Aldershot in front of a packed Anfield crowd. It is the start of an FA Cup journey that will end in a 2-1 defeat to Arsenal in the final some five months later.

MONDAY 2nd JANUARY 1978

A Steve Heighway goal ten minutes from time seals a routine victory for Liverpool over Middlesbrough at Anfield. It was one of 24 wins for Bob Paisley's side, who went on to finish second, seven points behind eventual winners Nottingham Forest – managed by Brian Clough. Liverpool were in a good run of form at the time, having lost only once in their previous eight games. David Johnson opened the scoring with his first goal of the season, and Kevin Kewley made his debut when he came on as a substitute for Terry McDermott after ten minutes.

SATURDAY 2nd JANUARY 1982

John Toshack receives a warm reception from the travelling Liverpool fans for the FA Cup third-round tie with his Swansea City side, but the niceties are put to one side once the game kicks off with the Reds unceremoniously beating the South Wales outfit 4-0. Alan Hansen, Ian Rush (2) and Mark Lawrenson score the goals in front of a packed Vetch Field crowd of 24,179.

SATURDAY 3rd JANUARY 1903

Thomas Green scores on his Liverpool debut away to Blackburn Rovers. Green made seven league appearances for the club and his only goal for Liverpool was scored in the second minute of his first match for the club. Despite his early strike, the Reds went down 3-1 on the day. Green moved on to Stockport County where he scored 16 goals in 23 league appearances in the 1904/05 season in the Midland League.

SATURDAY 3rd JANUARY 1948

Liverpool can't break down a dogged Stoke City resulting in a frustrating 0-0 draw at Anfield. The point leaves Liverpool in mid-table and the Potters four points clear of the relegation zone.

SATURDAY 3rd JANUARY 2009

Facing a tricky-looking tie at Deepdale, the Reds ease into the last 32 of the FA Cup thanks to a spectacular goal from Spanish winger Albert Riera in the first half, and a Fernando Torres strike in second-half injury time.

SATURDAY 4th JANUARY 1902

Skilful Scottish forward Andy McGuigan becomes the first Liverpool player to score five goals in a league game, at home to Stoke City. He later became a club director at Anfield, serving on the club's board when Liverpool won the championship two years in a row in 1922 and 1923.

SATURDAY 5th JANUARY 1946

Inside-forward Kevin Baron makes his Reds debut during a 2-0 FA Cup third-round victory over Chester. Baron had played as an amateur for his home-town club Preston North End before arriving at the club and he didn't really establish himself at Anfield until the 1949/50 campaign when he only missed four league matches and played in the FA Cup Final XI against Arsenal at Wembley.

SATURDAY 6th JANUARY 1962

A first-half goal avalanche eventually proves enough to see off a plucky Chelsea side in a thrilling 4-3 FA Cup third-round victory at Anfield. Ian St John grabs the Reds' first on 16 minutes and Roger Hunt adds a second on 28. St John and Alan A'Court add further strikes on 41 and 44 to lead 4-1 at half-time. But, the Londoners make a fist of the game after the break, almost forcing a replay in front of 48,455 breathless fans.

SATURDAY 7th JANUARY 2006

A Liverpool fan wins £25,000 after predicting Xabi Alonso would score from his own half during the 2005/06 campaign. Adrian Hayward placed £200 at 125-1 after watching the Spaniard go close to achieving the feat several times the previous season. Hayward said: "I've been a Liverpool supporter for 26 years and I noticed last season that Alonso attempted shooting from his own half quite a few times. I couldn't get it out of my head that he would eventually manage to get one."

XABI ALONSO SCORES ONE OF HIS 'SPECIALS', WINNING ONE FAN £25K (SEE 7TH JANUARY 2006).

SATURDAY 7th JANUARY 2006

Liverpool break Luton Town's hearts in what proves to be an FA Cup classic at Kenilworth Road. Steven Gerrard curls the Reds ahead but Luton recover to take a shock 2-1 lead when Steve Howard, and then Steve Robinson, drag the Hatters back into the game. Then, after a Djibril Cisse penalty miss, Kevin Nicholls' spot-kick made it 3-1 with the Berkshire side seemingly on the way to a major FA Cup shock. Florent Sinama Pongolle reduces the arrears just past the hour and Xabi Alonso levels scores seven minutes later with a 40-yard lob to make it 3-3 and Pongolle restores the Reds' lead on 73 minutes. The best was yet to come when Alonso caps off a memorable day with a 60-yard shot from his own half that gave Beresford no chance on 90 minutes to cap a fine all-round display and complete a 5-3 win.

SATURDAY 8th JANUARY 2011

Roy Hodgson leaves the club by mutual consent, with Liverpool struggling for form in the league. The former Fulham manager won just 13 of his 31 games in charge and was heavily criticised by fans following a 1-0 defeat at home to bottom-of-the-table Wolverhampton Wanderers, the first defeat to the Molineux side in 27 years. However, that was not the most embarrassing loss Hodgson would suffer as Liverpool boss. On Wednesday 22nd September 2010, he saw his side dumped out of the League Cup on penalties by League Two minnows Northampton Town following a 2-2 draw at Anfield.

SATURDAY 8th JANUARY 2011

Kenny Dalglish is re-appointed Liverpool manager after the club dispense with Roy Hodgson's services. For supporters, it's the ideal solution to several years of disappointing performances with the spirit of LFC somehow lost over the previous decade. Initially, the appointment is only until the end of the season, but he is handed a war chest that sees the arrival of Luis Suarez and Andy Carroll at a cost of more than £50m. The Reds' late run for a Europa League spot and improved league form make Dalglish's appointment on a permanent basis a formality a few months later.

TUESDAY 9th JANUARY 2007

There are not many teams who score six goals at Anfield and there are even fewer strikers who manage to score four goals away to the Reds – but that's exactly what happened as Arsenal won this League Cup quarter-final encounter 6-3 with Julio Baptista scoring four for the Gunners. Jeremie Aliadiere put the visitors 1-0 up and Robbie Fowler equalised, but a Baptista brace and Alex Song strike meant it was 4-1 by half-time – unheard of! Baptista added the club's fifth and after substitute Steven Gerrard, and Sami Hyypia, pulled two goals back, all hopes of a famous comeback were ended as the Brazilian made it six to seal a place in the semi-final, where the Gunners saw off Tottenham Hotspur – but lost to Chelsea in the final.

SUNDAY 9th JANUARY 2011

King Kenny begins his second spell in charge with a tough FA Cup third-round tie away to Manchester United – and sees his team fall behind in the first few seconds to a controversial penalty. Ryan Giggs scores the only goal of the game with just two minutes on the clock.

SATURDAY 10th JANUARY 1976

Six goals are shared at Anfield as Ipswich Town come away with a point, despite an early goal from Kevin Keegan. The England international got his seventh goal of the season after 13 minutes, before adding a second 20 minutes later. Jimmy Case salvaged a point for Bob Paisley's team when he scored with a little over ten minutes to go as both teams shared the spoils in a thrilling encounter. It was an impressive season for the Tractor Boys as they finished the campaign in sixth place, whereas Liverpool won their ninth English championship – one point ahead of Queens Park Rangers.

SATURDAY 10th JANUARY 2004

With half the season complete, a 38th-minute Mark Delaney own goal gives Liverpool a 1-0 win over Aston Villa at Anfield – but the Reds still trail joint leaders Arsenal and Manchester United by 17 points!

FRIDAY 11th JANUARY 2008

Czech defender Martin Skrtel becomes the most expensive defender in Liverpool's history when he joins the Reds in 2008 on a four-and-a-half-year contract for a transfer fee of £6.5 million. Boss Rafa Benitez says of the former Zenit St Petersburg star: "He is aggressive, quick, is good in the air and I think he's a very good player for the future and also for the present. He is very competitive, but his mentality for me is very good."

SATURDAY 12th JANUARY 2008

Fernando Torres rescues a point for Liverpool with a 71st-minute equaliser away to Middlesbrough. George Boateng had given the Teessiders the lead and the draw is good enough to put the Reds back up to fourth, though still 12 points adrift of leaders Manchester United.

SATURDAY 13th JANUARY 2001

Danny Murphy scores twice, and Steven Gerrard also bags a goal, as Liverpool beat Aston Villa 3-0 at Villa Park. The win keeps the Reds in fourth spot in the Premier League, 13 points off the top, but only three points behind second-place Sunderland.

SATURDAY 14th JANUARY 1899

The Reds' title hopes take a blow with a 0-0 draw away to Wolverhampton Wanderers. Though Liverpool remain fourth in Division One, they trail leaders Aston Villa by four points with the Midlands side also having three games in hand. Only 7,000 people attend the game and the Reds return to winning ways a week later with a 2-0 win over Everton.

WEDNESDAY 14th JANUARY 1981

Liverpool withstand fierce pressure to take a vital 1-0 lead in the first leg of the League Cup semi-final away to Manchester City. The Blues seemed to have scored a perfectly legitimate goal through Kevin Reeves but referee Alf Grey spotted an infringement the majority of the 48,085 Maine Road crowd didn't agree with. In a classic smash and grab, Ray Kennedy nicks an 81st-minute winner to put the Reds within sight of Wembley once again.

THURSDAY 15th JANUARY 1959

A day to forget for Liverpool FC as non-league Worcester City knock the Reds out of the FA Cup. With the original date for the cup tie postponed due to a frozen pitch, the re-arranged match was played in front of 15,111 fans the following Thursday – and after just nine minutes, Worcester were ahead when Tommy Skus scored the opening goal. The Reds couldn't stamp any authority on the game and on 80 minutes Worcester doubled their lead when Dick White put past his own keeper in bizarre fashion to make it 2-0. Geoff Twentyman pulled one back from the spot three minutes later, but it was too little, too late.

TUESDAY 16th JANUARY 1973

John Toshack scores his 15th and 16th goals of the season as Liverpool ease through their FA Cup third-round replay with Burnley. The initial tie finished 0-0 at Turf Moor, but 56,124 fans were treated to three goals at Anfield as Peter Cormack added to the two that Wales international Toshack had scored. The Clarets were hoping for a potential upset on Merseyside, but the eventual Division Two champions were comfortably dismantled by the eventual Division One champions.

WEDNESDAY 16th JANUARY 1985

Polish midfielder Zbigniew Boniek scores twice for Juventus in Turin as Giovanni Trapattoni's side beat Liverpool 2-0 in the European Super Cup. Originally, the game is to be played over two legs, but due to fixture congestion, the clubs agree to play just the one leg, which meant there was no tie at Anfield and no second chance for Joe Fagan's side.

SATURDAY 16th JANUARY 1999

Liverpool turn on the style as they thrash Southampton 7-1 at Anfield. The Reds don't score the first goal until the 22nd minute and the last goal is scored on 73 minutes, meaning all seven goals come in a 51-minute period! Robbie Fowler scores a hat-trick and Dominic Matteo, Jamie Carragher, Michael Owen and David Thompson all score one each to put the Reds sixth in the Premier League.

MONDAY 17th JANUARY 1921

Liverpool humble Arsenal 4-1 at Highbury in an FA Cup third-round replay. Harry Chambers scores twice, and Dick Johnson and Donald Mackinlay score the others, in an emphatic victory in north London.

SATURDAY 18th JANUARY 1969

Roger Hunt breaks the club record for league goals scored, overtaking Gordon Hodgson's previous tally when he bags another in a 2-1 win at Chelsea. Hunt was the Reds' top goalscorer eight years in a row from 1962 to 1969 and his league tally of 245 goals is still an LFC record. Hunt was knighted in 2000, though he observed it was just being made official as he had been called 'Sir Roger', by the Kop for a quarter of a century!

SUNDAY 19th JANUARY 1969

Steve Staunton is born in Drogheda, Ireland. Staunton was signed by Kenny Dalglish in September 1986 for £20,000 from Dundalk and won the FA Cup and league title in his first spell at Anfield. Graeme Souness sold him to Aston Villa on August 7th, 1991 and Staunton developed into one of the best left full-backs in the country. Once Roy Evans had taken over at Anfield in 1994, Staunton was linked with a return to Liverpool almost every single year. Finally, when he arrived on July 3rd, 1998 he had obviously left his best years behind him at Villa whom he eventually re-joined in 2000.

SATURDAY 20th JANUARY 2000

Boos ring out around Anfield as lowly Middlesbrough leave Merseyside with a point following a dour 0-0 draw. It's only the third time the Reds have failed to win a home game during the 1999/2000 campaign but is disappointing nonetheless for the capacity crowd who had envisaged a victory.

WEDNESDAY 20th JANUARY 2010

Dirk Kuyt scores twice to boost Liverpool's hopes of Champions League football in a 2-0 win over top-four rivals Tottenham Hotspur at Anfield. The Dutch striker scores after six minutes and seals the points with an injury-time penalty to close the gap on Harry Redknapp's men to just one point.

THURSDAY 21st JANUARY 1954

Future skipper Phil Thompson is born in Liverpool. After signing for the Reds during Bill Shankly's tenure, Thompson went on to play more than 300 times for the team he supported as a boy and became one of the most decorated players in English football history. He captained Liverpool from 1979 to 1982 and was England's captain for a spell, too. He joined Sheffield United in March 1985, bringing down the curtain on a fantastic Anfield career, though he returned twice as a coach.

TUESDAY 22nd JANUARY 2002

Danny Murphy sends 3,000 travelling Liverpool fans wild with an 85th-minute winner at Old Trafford. The 1-0 win over Manchester United closes the gap at the top of the Premier League to just two points and pushes the Reds into third spot.

SATURDAY 23rd JANUARY 1988

Liverpool, undefeated in the first 23 games of the campaign, beat Charlton 2-0 at The Valley to extend their lead over closest rivals Nottingham Forest to an astonishing 17 points with only 24 games played.

SATURDAY 24th JANUARY 1970

Liverpool progress safely to the fifth round of the FA Cup after a 3-1 victory over Wrexham at Anfield. More than 54,000 spectators watch Bill Shankly's team overcome the tricky Third Division opposition. All of Liverpool's goals came in the second half, with Bobby Graham getting his 16th goal of the season six minutes after the interval. Ian St John bagged his seventh goal of the season just eight minutes later, before Graham netted his second to secure a comfortable passage through to the next round.

SATURDAY 25th JANUARY 1930

Tom Bradshaw his makes club debut in a 1-0 win over Manchester United at Anfield. Nicknamed 'Tiny', Bradshaw stood at just over six feet two inches and was a veteran of 208 league games with Bury. Tiny played in the last 17 league matches of the 1929/30 season and though he was used as a wing-half in his debut season, he was just as comfortable at centre-half, a position he made his own over the next seven seasons. Bradshaw went on to clock up almost 300 first-team appearances for the Reds, who were at a low ebb for most of the time he was with the club.

PHIL THOMPSON – LIKE A STICK OF ROCK HE HAS LIVERPOOL FC RUNNING THROUGH HIS BODY (SEE 21ST JANUARY 1954).

WEDNESDAY 26th JANUARY 1994

After 97 appearances and 22 goals, popular Israeli striker Ronny Rosenthal joins Tottenham Hotspur for £250,000. Rosenthal had slipped out of the first-team picture during the 1994/95 campaign and some supporters – mostly at other clubs – couldn't forget his astonishing miss away to Aston Villa when he thundered a shot against the bar from a few yards out with the keeper stranded. Ironically, his transfer went through just 48 hours before Graeme Souness resigned as Liverpool boss, but it was two days too late for Ronny.

FRIDAY 27th JANUARY 2006

Robbie Fowler returns to Liverpool on a free transfer from Manchester City. The striker the fans call 'God' left for Leeds United before joining City, but never re-discovered the form that made him an Anfield legend. Five days after re-signing for the Reds, he came on as a substitute for Peter Crouch in a home game with Birmingham City and the five goals he managed to score before the end of the season earned him an additional one-year deal. He managed seven more goals before joining Cardiff City in July 2007 having scored 183 goals in 369 appearances for the Reds.

FRIDAY 28th JANUARY 1994

Former Liverpool midfielder Graeme Souness, who won three European Cups and five league championships in his time as a player at Anfield, is only the second manager in the club's history to be sacked following a humiliating FA Cup exit at the hands of Division Two outfit Bristol City. Liverpool fans had begun to lose patience with the Scot, having only managed to bring one FA Cup to Merseyside in his three years at the helm. However, his legacy was plain to see as he brought through Steve McManaman, Robbie Fowler and Jamie Redknapp in 1992, before purchasing David James from Watford.

WEDNESDAY 28th JANUARY 2009

Yossi Benayoun's 41st-minute goal looks enough to have given Liverpool three points at Wigan Athletic before Egyptian striker Mido equalises from the penalty spot just seven minutes from time to earn the hosts a share of the spoils. The dropped points mean the Reds miss the chance to top the Premier League while Wigan move up to seventh in the table.

SATURDAY 29th JANUARY 1938

The Reds' hopes of avoiding relegation take a blow following a 0-0 draw against Grimsby Town at Blundell Park. The Mariners, just two places and two points ahead of 21st-placed Liverpool, are one of 14 teams separated by just six points.

TUESDAY 30th JANUARY 1951

The Reds lose another manager to ill health in the shape of George Kay, who spent 15 years in charge of the club, although his time at the helm was interrupted by the outbreak of World War II. Kay could only lead the club to one league title during his tenure in the 1946/47 campaign, where his side won 2-1 against Wolverhampton Wanderers at Molineux. Sadly, Kay died just three months later.

SATURDAY 30th JANUARY 1971

John Toshack scores a fourth-minute goal to get Liverpool off to a flyer in a top-of-the-table clash with Arsenal at Anfield. The Welshman scored his fifth goal of the season before defender Tommy Smith got his third goal of the season – the 32nd of his Liverpool career – five minutes after the interval. The result would be a minor blip in the Gunners' season as they went on to lift the Division One title for the eighth time, while Bill Shankly's Liverpool side could only manage a fifth-place finish, finishing 14 points behind Arsenal.

WEDNESDAY 30th JANUARY 2002

Abel Xavier becomes only the second Everton player of recent times to take the short trip across Stanley Park to join Liverpool. Xavier played in seven countries including Portugal, the Netherlands, Italy, Spain, England, Turkey and the USA and though he didn't score during his time at Goodison Park, he netted on his debut for the Reds against Ipswich Town, one of just 14 appearances before he was loaned out to Galatasaray.

SATURDAY 31st JANUARY 1948

A miserable afternoon at Anfield as Portsmouth beat the Reds 3-0. It's one of five successive defeats for Liverpool and will be one of three consecutive 3-0 defeats in a campaign that sees the club finish 11th in Division One.

SATURDAY 31st JANUARY 1976

With Liverpool and West Ham United still locked at 0-0 with over an hour gone at Upton Park, few among the 26,741 fans could have envisaged what was about to happen. In the final 27 minutes, the Reds stepped up a gear and John Toshack scored a hat-trick with Kevin Keegan adding a late fourth to give Bob Paisley's side an impressive victory and a ninth game without defeat on the way to the title.

WEDNESDAY 31st JANUARY 2001

Manchester City had won once in 11 games and Liverpool had won 11 times in their previous 15, so the odds appeared heavily stacked in the Reds' favour for this Premier League clash at Maine Road. Yet despite the Reds taking the lead through Emile Heskey on 43 minutes, struggling City levelled just two minutes after the break when Danny Tiatto levelled for the Blues, who would lose their top-flight status at the end of the season.

MONDAY 31st JANUARY 2011

Andy Carroll signs for Liverpool for a club record £35m from Newcastle United. Carroll's fledgling career began with four Premier League appearances for the Magpies in 2006/07, in addition to becoming the club's youngest-ever participant in a competitive European fixture when he played against Palermo in a Uefa Cup tie early in November, 2006. He steadily rose to prominence at St James' Park and in 2009/10, he bagged 17 goals as Newcastle regained their top-flight status. He scored another 11 goals before joining the Reds in the January transfer window.

MONDAY 31st JANUARY 2011

Fernando Torres leaves Liverpool in a deal worth more than £40m – double the fee he was bought for. The Reds had resisted Chelsea's overtures for several months, but the Spaniard's dip in form, coupled with new boss Kenny Dalglish's desire for a new-look strike force, meant it was time for 'El Nino' to move on. Signed from Atletico Madrid in 2007, Torres quickly became a huge hit on Merseyside and settled into English football seamlessly. His 81 goals in 142 appearances ensure he will always be a favourite of the Liverpool supporters.

LIVERPOOL FC
On This Day

FEBRUARY

SATURDAY 1st FEBRUARY 1964

Ian St John hits a hat-trick as Liverpool run riot with a 6-1 victory over Sheffield United at Anfield. The win puts the Reds three points off the top of Division One with the other goals coming from Roger Hunt (2) and Peter Thompson.

SUNDAY 1st FEBRUARY 2009

Fernando Torres scores twice in the final two minutes against Chelsea to give Liverpool the win. The Spanish number nine headed home at the near post in the 88th minute, before going on to net again 90 seconds later after Yossi Benayoun had got the better of Ashley Cole. The win takes Rafa Benitez's side into second place and within two points of the Premier League summit.

SATURDAY 2nd FEBRUARY 1935

Gordon Hodgson hits a hat-trick as Liverpool beat Leeds United 4-2 at Anfield. The Reds scored three times in the final ten minutes, after Hodgson had got his first goal just after the quarter-hour mark. The South African striker went on to convert chances in the 84th and 87th minutes, with Alf Hanson getting the other.

SATURDAY 2nd FEBRUARY 1952

Anfield houses a record gate of 61,905 for the visit of Wolverhampton Wanderers in the FA Cup fourth round. The vast majority leave smiling with a 2-1 win putting Liverpool into the last 16 of the competition.

SATURDAY 2nd FEBRUARY 2008

Liverpool score three second-half goals to beat Sunderland 3-0 at Anfield and put Rafa Benitez's side into fifth, a point behind fourth-placed Everton. Peter Crouch breaks the deadlock on 57 minutes and Fernando Torres doubles the Reds' lead 12 minutes later. Steven Gerrard completes the scoring with an 89th-minute penalty.

WEDNESDAY 2nd FEBRUARY 2006

Steven Gerrard's second-half goal is enough to earn Liverpool a 1-1 draw at lowly Birmingham, losing further ground on the leading clubs above them.

WEDNESDAY 2nd FEBRUARY 2011

Just two days after signing from Ajax, Luis Suarez scores on his Liverpool debut as the Reds beat Stoke City 2-0 at Anfield. Raul Meireles opens the scoring on 47 minutes before second-half sub Suarez becomes an instant hit with a scuffed effort on 79 minutes to send the home fans wild.

SATURDAY 3rd FEBRUARY 2001

Liverpool beat West Ham United 3-0 at Anfield. Vladimir Smicer scores the first after 20 minutes, before Robbie Fowler bags a brace to overcome the Hammers. The Liverpool midfield trio played a key role in the game, with Igor Biscan, Didi Hamann and Steven Gerrard nullifying the visitors' threat.

SUNDAY 3rd FEBRUARY 2002

Liverpool move within two points of leaders Manchester United with a stunning 4-0 victory over Leeds United at Elland Road. Leading 1-0 thanks to Rio Ferdinand's first-half own goal, Emile Heskey scores two in two minutes, just past the hour, to make it 3-0 and Michael Owen rubs salt in the Lilywhites' wounds with a fourth on 90 minutes.

SATURDAY 4th FEBRUARY 1984

Liverpool remain five points clear of the pack after a 0-0 draw away to lowly Sunderland. Though disappointing, nearest challengers Manchester United fail to take advantage of the Reds' slip as they also drop two points after a 0-0 draw with Norwich City at Old Trafford.

WEDNESDAY 4th FEBRUARY 2009

Everton score a late winner to advance to the next round of the FA Cup at Liverpool's expense following a replay. Many of those watching at home miss the goal as ITV go to an advert break in the middle of the coverage.

WEDNESDAY 5th FEBRUARY 1977

John Toshack nets twice for Liverpool in a 4-1 win over Birmingham City at Anfield in a First Division clash. The Welshman's goals were sandwiched between a Phil Neal penalty in the 37th minute, and a late goal from Steve Heighway in front of 41,072 fans.

SATURDAY 5th FEBRUARY 2000

Dietmar Hamann scores his first Liverpool goal in a 3-1 victory over Leeds United at Anfield. Patrik Berger and Danny Murphy are also on target but the tall German midfielder's goal gets the loudest cheer. It will be one of only 11 goals in 283 appearances for the Reds before he joins Manchester City.

SUNDAY 6th FEBRUARY 1916

Jack Balmer is born in Liverpool. After a spell at Everton as an amateur, the forward arrives at Anfield in 1935 where he stays for the next 17 years, with his career being halted by the outbreak of war. He goes on to make 309 appearances for the club, scoring 110 times in the process. In 1946 he scores three hat-tricks in as many games to set a Football League record.

TUESDAY 6th FEBRUARY 2007

American tycoons George Gillett and Tom Hicks reach an agreement to take over Liverpool FC. The pair, who each own NHL ice hockey teams, become co-chairmen, leaving chief executive Rick Parry to run the club. Current Liverpool chairman David Moores, who became an honorary life president, said: "This is a great step forward for its shareholders and its fans." Gillett and Hicks beat off competition from Dubai International Capital to buy the Reds.

SATURDAY 7th FEBRUARY 1953

Teenager Alan A'Court, 18, makes his Liverpool debut in a 3-2 win away to Middlesbrough. The Rainhill-born left winger soon becomes a regular fixture in the first team and earns a reputation for spectacular goals thanks to his explosive shooting power. A'Court goes on to make 381 appearances during an 11-year period for the Reds, scoring 63 goals, before joining Preston North End in 1964.

SATURDAY 7th FEBRUARY 1976

The telepathic duo of Kevin Keegan and John Toshack strike again as the Reds beat Leeds United 2-0 at Anfield. Keegan scores the opener after four minutes and Toshack seals the points on 71 minutes.

DIETMAR HAMANN HAMMERS HIS FIRST LIVERPOOL GOAL (SEE 5TH FEBRUARY 2000).

SATURDAY 7th FEBRUARY 2009

Despite Portsmouth leading twice in the game, Liverpool came out on the right side of a 3-2 result at Anfield. Fernando Torres scores a last-minute winner to give the home side the points. Fabio Aurelio was the first to pull the Reds level in the 69th minute, and Dirk Kuyt netted with only six minutes left on the clock before Torres' heroics.

SATURDAY 8th FEBRUARY 1913

Two Jack Robinson goals give Liverpool a 2-0 win over Everton at Goodison Park. More than 40,000 people watch the Division One Merseyside derby and Robinson strikes in the 26th and 70th minutes and the Reds join the Blues in tenth spot as a result, with identical goal average records unable to separate the two great rivals.

SATURDAY 8th FEBRUARY 1975

A goal feast as Liverpool win 5-2 against Ipswich Town at Anfield. John Toshack scores twice for the Reds in front of 47,421 fans, with the other goals coming from Brian Hall, Peter Cormack and a rare strike from wing-half Alec Lindsay, enough to give Liverpool the points.

SATURDAY 9th FEBRUARY 1901

John Robertson becomes the first Liverpool player to be sent off when he is ordered to take an early bath by the referee during a 2-0 FA Cup first-round defeat at Notts County. Robertson plays 47 times for the Reds during his two-year stay on Merseyside.

SATURDAY 9th FEBRUARY 2002

Both Michael Owen and Emile Heskey net twice each, as Liverpool demolish Ipswich 6-0 at Portman Road. Abel Xavier scores the first in the 16th minute, with Heskey doubling the lead just before half-time. There is no let-up in the second period, as Sami Hyypia finds the back of the net, with Owen getting his brace, and Heskey getting another in the final minute. The margin of victory is enough to take the Reds to the top of the Premier League, despite previous leaders Newcastle United also winning that day, 3-1.

SUNDAY 10th FEBRUARY 1992

Ivan Kozma joins the Reds at a cost of £300,000 from Dunfermline Athletic. The Hungarian star was a skilful player who impressed boss Graeme Souness during his time as Rangers boss, but he found the pace of English football a different proposition altogether and would play just ten times during a disappointing 14-month spell at Anfield.

SATURDAY 10th FEBRUARY 2001

Striker Jari Litmanen scores his first goal for the club since arriving from FC Barcelona on a free transfer in a 1-1 draw at the Stadium of Light. The Finnish forward slots a penalty home with a little over ten minutes left on the clock, having come on as a first-half substitute for Emile Heskey.

SATURDAY 11th FEBRUARY 1933

Liverpool beat Everton 7-4 in the highest scoring Merseyside derby of all time. Toffees legend Dixie Dean led the line for Everton, scoring twice, but a hat-trick from Harold Barton saw the home side romp to victory in this 11-goal epic. The victory was sweet revenge for the 3-1 defeat suffered at Goodison Park earlier in the season – a game the Reds had led 1-0 at half-time in.

SATURDAY 11th FEBRUARY 1961

Dave Hickson hits a hat-trick for Liverpool as they demolish Leyton Orient 5-0 at Anfield. Hickson nets after just five minutes and the home side have a three-goal advantage going into the interval thanks to a strike from John Morrissey, and Hickson's second. Hickson completes his triple with ten minutes to go, before Kevin Lewis adds the fifth to rub yet more salt in the Londoners' wounds.

THURSDAY 11th FEBRUARY 1972

Steve McManaman is born in Bootle. The boyhood Everton fan joins the Reds aged 14 and makes his debut in 1990 – the start of almost a decade of first-team action for Liverpool during which 'Macca' clocked up 364 appearances and scored 66 goals. He left Anfield for Real Madrid and finished his playing career with Manchester City, though he never reached his previous heights with either club.

MONDAY 12th FEBRUARY 1923

From hero to zero. With Liverpool sitting comfortably atop the Football League, David Ashworth leaves the club to return to Oldham, where he had been manager for eight years from 1906 to 1914. Oldham were propping up the rest of the league and ended up being relegated that season, while the Reds finished six points clear to end the campaign as champions, despite winning only one of their remaining seven games. It was a surprising resignation as Ashworth had led the club to the Division One title the previous season.

SATURDAY 12th FEBRUARY 1975

Liverpool are given a rare thrashing as Newcastle United romp home 4-1 against the Reds at St James' Park. Brian Hall scores the visitors' only goal as Liverpool's title ambitions take a serious blow. Though still two points off the top, the Reds drop to fifth in the table with Everton in first.

TUESDAY 12th FEBRUARY 1985

Seventh-placed Liverpool stroll to a 3-0 win over Arsenal in a First Division clash at Anfield. Ian Rush scores the opener in the 32nd minute. It would take another 20 minutes for the Reds to double their advantage as Phil Neal gets the second before Ronnie Whelan completes the scoring late on.

SATURDAY 13th FEBRUARY 1904

New signing Robbie Robinson makes his debut during a 0-0 draw with Stoke City. The hard-working forward had once scored 132 goals in one season as a schoolboy and arrived with a lofty reputation he soon proved correct with the Reds. Robinson would remain on Merseyside until 1912 and moved into defence in his later years as a Liverpool player. He played 271 times in total, scoring 65 goals before joining Tranmere Rovers.

SATURDAY 13th FEBRUARY 1988

A Peter Beardsley brace inspires Liverpool to a 4-1 win over Watford at Anfield. The forward gets his first in the 29th minute, with John Aldridge doubling the lead early in the second half. It is Beardsley who adds the third, with the former Watford man John Barnes completing the scoring on the hour mark.

WEDNESDAY 14th FEBRUARY 1996

Bob Paisley dies aged 77. Without doubt Liverpool's most successful manager and one of the greatest of all time, Paisley would be the first to admit Bill Shankly's influence ran through his team like a rich vein of gold. An incredible manager who somehow bettered even Shankly's record with a glorious period of trophies, titles and unsurpassed supremacy, yet despite this, you'd have been hard pressed to find a more humble, good-natured man. Paisley polished the diamonds coming through the Anfield youth system and spent wisely when he had to – Graeme Souness, Kenny Dalglish and Alan Hansen proved to be the backbone of the team during the mid-to-late 1970s and were all signed by Paisley. A lovely man with a wry sense of humour, he may not have been keen to move into the spotlight but he grew to love his role as boss of the best team in Europe.

SATURDAY 14th FEBRUARY 1987

Ian Rush nets a hat-trick in an enthralling 4-3 victory over Leicester City. The first is scored by Paul Walsh, before Rush comes into his own as he scores in the 39th, 47th and 86th minutes to give Liverpool the points. Craig Johnston netted an own goal in the game, but this wasn't enough to save the Foxes.

WEDNESDAY 15th FEBRUARY 1928

Poor health eventually leads to the retirement of Matt McQueen after five years in charge of the club. He was the first former player to become manager of Liverpool after taking the job on a temporary basis following the resignation of Ashworth. McQueen was forced to retire after losing a leg whilst en route to Sheffield to do a scouting mission. One of his most significant signings was that of Gordon Hodgson. The South African scored just shy of 250 senior goals in less than 400 appearances.

WEDNESDAY 15th FEBRUARY 1995

A last-gasp Robbie Fowler strike gives Liverpool a slight advantage going into the second leg of their League Cup semi-final tie with Crystal Palace. The forward scores in the final minute of the match, which is rightly deserved after Liverpool dominate the game from start to finish, earning 17 corners in the process.

WEDNESDAY 15th FEBRUARY 2001

Liverpool put one foot into the Uefa Cup quarter-finals with a 2-0 first-leg win away to AS Roma at the Stadio Olimpico – scene of two LFC European Cup triumphs. Two second-half Michael Owen goals – the first in the 46th, the second after 71 minutes – mean the second leg at Anfield is all but a formality – or so everyone thought! Roma push the Reds all the way in the return game, winning 1-0 and narrowly going out 2-1 on aggregate.

SATURDAY 16th FEBRUARY 1963

Kevin Lewis and Ian St John both net twice as Liverpool ease past Wolverhampton Wanderers at Anfield. More than 50,000 people witness the Reds' 4-1 victory. Liverpool are dominant from the word go with Lewis scoring in the seventh minute, but it took another 40 until St John got the second, after which Lewis doubled his tally on 53 and St John completed the scoring three minutes from time.

SATURDAY 16th FEBRUARY 2008

The Reds' hopes of FA Cup glory are dashed in a hugely disappointing 2-1 home defeat to Championship outfit Barnsley. Having already stuttered against Luton Town and Havant & Waterlooville, Liverpool's penchant for nearly shooting themselves in the foot finally found its target. Dirk Kuyt put Rafa Benitez's men 1-0 up, but Stephen Foster and an injury-time winner from Brian Howard, put the Tykes through to the quarter-finals rather than the hosts.

SATURDAY 17th FEBRUARY 1990

Liverpool brush aside Southampton in an FA Cup fifth-round tie at Anfield. The heroes on the day are Ian Rush, Peter Beardsley and Steve Nicol who guarantee Liverpool's progression to the next round by netting three unanswered goals against the Saints in front of 35,961 fans.

SATURDAY 17th FEBRUARY 1991

Liverpool are held to a goalless draw in the FA Cup fifth round by Everton in a feisty Merseyside derby. The Toffees are denied a first-ever FA Cup win at Anfield when Pat Nevin is floored in the box by Gary Ablett on 39 minutes – but no penalty is awarded.

PETER BEARDSLEY – FULL OF TRICKERY AND GUILE (SEE 17TH FEBRUARY 1990).

THURSDAY 17th FEBRUARY 2011

Liverpool secure a valuable 0-0 draw in the first leg of the Europa League Round of 32. Less than 18,000 witness the match away to Sparta Rotterdam as the Reds pursue their last hope of silverware in what used to be known as the Uefa Cup.

SATURDAY 18th FEBRUARY 2001

Liverpool dismantle a poor Manchester City side at Anfield in a 4-2 victory. Jari Litmanen and Emile Heskey put the hosts 2-0 up inside 13 minutes before Andrei Kanchelskis pulls one back on 29 minutes for City. Vladimir Smicer makes it 3-1 from the spot on 54 minutes and Markus Babbel completes the rout five minutes from time before Shaun Goater grabs a consolation in injury time.

WEDNESDAY 18th FEBRUARY 2006

Liverpool beat Manchester United 1-0 in the FA Cup. Peter Crouch scores the only goal of the game in the 18th minute. The giant striker heads home a Steve Finnan cross after giving marker Nemanja Vidic a torrid time.

TUESDAY 19th FEBRUARY 1997

Stan Collymore hits two as Liverpool defeat Leeds United 4-0 at Anfield. The strikes sandwiched a Robbie Fowler goal in the 21st minute and a Jamie Redknapp finish late on. Collymore's goals came within two minutes of each other just after the half hour mark.

WEDNESDAY 19th FEBRUARY 2008

Liverpool take a 2-0 lead over Inter Milan in the first leg of the first knockout round of the Champions League. With the score 0-0 and with just five minutes left, goals from Dirk Kuyt and Steven Gerrard send Anfield wild – as well as giving Rafa Benitez's side a vital advantage in the tie.

SATURDAY 20th FEBRUARY 1909

Liverpool's title hopes take a fatal blow as lowly Woolwich Arsenal dish out a 5-0 hammering. The Reds slip to fifth as a result, while Arsenal move away from the relegation zone.

WEDNESDAY 20th FEBRUARY 1985

John Wark hits a hat-trick as Liverpool score seven unanswered goals against York City in an FA Cup fifth-round replay at Anfield. The others on the score-sheet are Ronnie Whelan who nets twice, Phil Neal and a late strike from Paul Walsh completes the rout.

WEDNESDAY 20th FEBRUARY 1991

A third Merseyside derby in a row as Liverpool and Everton battle it out for supremacy of the city. Having beaten the Toffees 3-1 in the league and then been held 0-0 in the FA Cup fifth round eight days later – both at Anfield – the two tribes went to war again in an epic match at Goodison Park. In a rollercoaster contest, Liverpool saw the lead slip from their grasp four times and a drained Dalglish resigned the morning after. The rare start 'King' Kenny Dalglish gave Peter Beardsley paid off with the England star scoring twice in normal time. Ian Rush, inevitably, also netted for the Reds, but a determined Everton equalised repeatedly, thanks to two from Graeme Sharp and one from Tony Cottee with three minutes remaining. John Barnes struck a superb curler in extra time, but Cottee managed a fourth equaliser to send the game to a second replay which Everton won 1-0 bringing to an end four Merseyside derbies in 18 frantic days.

SATURDAY 21st FEBRUARY 1979

Kenny Dalglish and David Johnson both score twice as Liverpool demolish Norwich City 6-0 at Anfield. The Scottish striker netted in the third minute, but the other five goals didn't come until the second half. Johnson got his first moments after the restart following the interval. It was soon four, as Dalglish and Johnson both doubled their tallies, before Alan and Ray Kennedy got a goal each.

SATURDAY 21st FEBRUARY 1988

Ray Houghton's 76th-minute winner sends Liverpool into the FA Cup semi-finals and Everton crashing out of the competition as the Reds triumph 1-0 at Goodison Park. The victory extends Kenny Dalglish's side's unbeaten run to 20 matches, though the cup adventure will end in disappointment with a 1-0 defeat to Wimbledon in the final three months later.

WEDNESDAY 21st FEBRUARY 2007

Goals from Craig Bellamy and John Arne Riise give Liverpool a famous 2-1 win over Barcelona at the Nou Camp in the first leg of the Champions League knockout stages. The Reds lose the return 1-0 at Anfield but still progress towards the Holy Grail...

FRIDAY 22nd FEBRUARY 1991

Kenny Dalglish resigns as Liverpool boss on health grounds. But for being banned in Europe during most of his reign, Dalglish could possibly have emulated his old manager Bob Paisley with his six years as Anfield chief the club's last real golden years of the modern era and how high the Reds may have flown under the tenure of 'King Kenny', one can only guess. One of Anfield's favourite sons, Dalglish managed to make the transition from player to boss smoothly but the tragic events of Hillsborough were ultimately too much to bear. His compassion to the bereaved families will always be remembered on Merseyside and, if anything, increased his standing even more among the Liverpool fans.

TUESDAY 22nd FEBRUARY 2005

Liverpool defeat Bayer Leverkusen 3-1 in the first leg of their Champions League tie. Luis Garcia opened the scoring after 15 minutes, before John Arne Riise doubled the lead later in the first half. Dietmar Hamann hits a free kick past the keeper in the final minute to put Liverpool almost out of sight, but a Jerzy Dudek error in injury time allows the Germans to pull one back giving them hope going into the second leg.

SATURDAY 23rd FEBRUARY 2002

Nicolas Anelka rescues a point for Liverpool after Tomasz Radzinski gives Everton a surprise lead at Anfield. The point does little for the Reds' title credentials but boosts the Toffees' survival hopes.

SUNDAY 23rd FEBRUARY 2003

Relegation-threatened Birmingham City cause a surprise as they beat Liverpool 2-1 at St Andrew's in a scrappy Premier League clash. Goals from Stephen Clemence and Clinton Morrison give the Blues a 2-0 lead before second-half substitute Michael Owen reduces the arrears with a late consolation goal.

SATURDAY 23rd FEBRUARY 2008

Fernando Torres produces a one-man show, as he scores all three in Liverpool's victory over Middlesbrough at Anfield. Liverpool concede first but a quick-fire double from Torres put his side ahead just before the half-hour mark. His final goal comes after a mix-up in the visitors' defence that allows the Spaniard to put the ball into an empty net and complete his treble.

FRIDAY 24th FEBRUARY 1987

Nigel Spackman joins Liverpool from Chelsea for a fee of £400,000. Spackman goes straight into the starting line-up the following day and goes on to play 63 times for the Reds in a two-year period before joining QPR after failing to nail down a regular starting place.

WEDNESDAY 25th FEBRUARY 1914

The Reds race in a 4-1 half-time lead in the FA Cup third-round replay with West Ham United. Lacey and Miller score two goals each before Metcalfe adds a fifth to send Liverpool into the fourth round.

SUNDAY 25th FEBRUARY 2001

Jamie Carragher is an unlikely hero as he scores the winning spot kick in the penalty shoot-out to ensure Liverpool win their first major trophy for six years – the League Cup. Robbie Fowler had given Liverpool the lead when he scored on the half-hour mark, and just as it was looking as though that would be enough, Stefan Henchoz brings down Martin O'Connor in the penalty area and Darren Purse confidently buries the resulting spot kick. Purse was on hand to convert in the shoot-out, but after Carragher scored in sudden death, Birmingham's Andy Johnson could not keep his nerve and Liverpool won the competition for the sixth time.

WEDNESDAY 25th FEBRUARY 2009

A late Yossi Benayoun goal gives Liverpool a one-goal lead in the first leg of their Champions League tie against Real Madrid. The Israeli silenced the Santiago Bernabéu in the 82nd minute by heading home a Fabio Aurelio free kick to give Rafa Benitez a victory over the team he supported as a boy.

SATURDAY 26th FEBRUARY 1972

Larry Lloyd, Kevin Keegan and Bobby Graham all score as Liverpool thrash fellow title challengers and league leaders Manchester City 3-0 at Anfield. It's City's first defeat in ten games and is revenge for the 1-0 defeat suffered at Maine Road earlier in the season and puts the Reds fifth in the table, just four points adrift of Joe Mercer's side.

THURSDAY 26th FEBRUARY 2004

Liverpool defeat Bulgarian outfit Levski Sofia in the Uefa Cup. Second-half goals from captain Steven Gerrard and Australian winger Harry Kewell give the Reds a deserved victory at Anfield and a vital edge going into the return leg in Eastern Europe.

THURSDAY 27th FEBRUARY 2003

Liverpool see off the tough challenge of French side Auxerre at Anfield in a Uefa Cup fourth-round tie. Michael Owen and Danny Murphy score midway through the second half, and the visitors had no response leaving Liverpool with a 2-0 lead, which saw the Reds progress having won by a single goal in France the previous week.

SUNDAY 27th FEBRUARY 2005

John Arne Riise gets Liverpool off to the perfect start in their tenth League Cup Final outing as he crashes home the opener with less than a minute played at the Millennium Stadium. But a Steven Gerrard own goal with ten minutes to go forces extra time during which Didier Drogba and Mateja Kežman score two goals in the space of five second period minutes to put Chelsea in a commanding position. Antonio Núñez pulls one back, but it is not enough for the Reds, who lose 3-2 in Rafael Benitez's first major final in charge of the club.

SATURDAY 28th FEBRUARY 1998

Brad Friedel makes his debut for Liverpool away to Aston Villa – his future employers. The American goalkeeper plays well, but despite Michael Owen scoring for the Reds after just six minutes, Villa hit back to win 2-1. Friedel plays just 31 times for Liverpool in three years before joining Blackburn Rovers and proving what an excellent keeper he is.

SATURDAY 28th FEBRUARY 2010

Liverpool defeat a resilient Blackburn Rovers team 2-1 at Anfield. Though the performance is disappointing, goals from Steven Gerrard and Fernando Torres are enough to see the Reds earn all three points. It was Torres' strike that makes the difference when he converted a cross from Maxi Rodriguez after Blackburn had fashioned an equaliser.

SATURDAY 29th FEBRUARY 1896

Liverpool beat Burton Swifts 7-0 to strengthen the Reds' lead at the top of Division Two. It's the first time the club has played a Leap Year game, and Ross and Becton both help themselves to a hat-trick while McCartney opens the scoring on 15 minutes for the free-scoring hosts. Liverpool clock up an amazing 107 goals in just 30 games on their way to the Division Two title.

SATURDAY 29th FEBRUARY 1956

Liverpool's 1-0 win over Leeds United puts the Reds within five points of leaders Sheffield Wednesday – despite being in eighth place. The winner is scored by prolific marksman John Evans in the 56th minute of this feisty Division Two clash.

SATURDAY 29th FEBRUARY 1992

Any lingering hopes Liverpool have of making a late title surge are finally ended after a toothless display against bottom side Southampton ends 0-0 at Anfield. The dropped points leave the Reds 13 points adrift of leaders Manchester United, though the visitors understandably celebrate the point with relish, breathing new life into their battle to beat the drop.

SUNDAY 29th FEBRUARY 2004

Harry Kewell scores on his return to Elland Road in a blood and thunder clash between Leeds and Liverpool. Kewell puts the Reds 1-0 up before two goals in five minutes from Eirik Bakke and Mark Viduka give the Lilywhites a 2-1 lead. Milan Baros equalises before the break to make it 2-2 at the break and there is no further scoring in the second half. The point is neither her nor there for the Reds who trail 'The Invincibles' Arsenal by 28 points while Leeds remain rooted to the foot of the table.

LIVERPOOL FC
On This Day

MARCH

TUESDAY 1st MARCH 1988

Sammy Lee is injured and misses his own testimonial as Liverpool beat Osasuna 2-0 at the El Sadar stadium in Spain. More than 12,000 turn out for the game and goals from Kenny Dalglish and Ray Houghton ensure Lee's big night is victorious. The team was: Grobbelaar, Ablett, Spackman, Nicol, Whelan (Watson), Hansen, Molby (MacDonald), Aldridge (Dalglish), Houghton, Barnes, McMahon.

WEDNESDAY 2nd MARCH 1977

Liverpool lose 1-0 to St Etienne in France in the third round, first leg European Cup tie. Though the Reds hold out until the break, the hosts score the only goal in the second period to take a narrow lead to Anfield. Facing elimination on the away goals rule despite leading 2-1 in the return leg, 'Super Sub' David Fairclough scores a late third to send Bob Paisley's side through 3-2 on aggregate and into the semi-final.

SUNDAY 2nd MARCH 2003

A late Michael Owen goal four minutes from time seals victory for Liverpool in the League Cup Final as they beat Manchester United 2-0 at the Millennium Stadium. Steven Gerrard puts the Reds in front six minutes before the interval – and on course for a seventh League Cup triumph – before Owen puts the game beyond doubt to give Gerard Houllier his sixth major trophy in charge of the club.

SATURDAY 3rd MARCH 1956

John Evans proves the scourge of Bury for a second successive season as he scores twice in a 4-2 win over the Shakers. Evans, who scored four against Bury almost exactly a year before, nets a fifth-minute penalty and adds another on 74 minutes with Billy Liddell also bagging a brace in front of 35,535 Anfield fans.

WEDNESDAY 3rd MARCH 1976

Bob Paisley's Liverpool hold Dynamo Dresden to a 0-0 draw in the first leg of the Uefa Cup quarter-final at the Rudolf Harbig Stadium in East Germany. The Reds have Ray Clemence to thank for the clean sheet after he saves a Peter Kotte penalty following a tip-off from Paisley.

TUESDAY 3rd MARCH 1998

Ally McCoist scores the only goal of the game as Rangers beat Liverpool 1-0 at Ibrox for Walter Smith's testimonial. Smith won the Scottish Premier League for seven consecutive seasons between 1990 and 1997, and also six domestic trophies, as he became one of the most successful managers in the club's history. Paul Ince, Steve McManaman and Michael Owen featured for the visitors, but were unable to find a goal on the night.

SATURDAY 4th MARCH 1939

A crowd of around 18,000 see an eight-goal thriller at Anfield as Liverpool and Portsmouth serve up a Saturday afternoon treat. In a topsy-turvy game, Liverpool never quite find the breathing space they need to seal the game, despite leading several times. Willie Fagan and Phil Taylor ensure the hosts go into the break 2-1 up, and Taylor and Berry Nieuwenhuys both add goals after the break, but a dogged Pompey refuse to throw the towel in and fully deserve the 4-4 draw they eventually get.

SATURDAY 4th MARCH 1967

One of Liverpool's greatest servants, Emlyn Hughes, makes his league debut in a 2-1 home win over Stoke City at Anfield. Signed by Bill Shankly for £65,000 from Blackpool, it's the start of an 11-year career spent almost entirely in the first team during which Hughes – nicknamed Crazy Horse – became one of the most successful skippers in the Reds' history. Hughes finally moved to Wolves in 1979 after 669 appearances. Hughes will also be long remembered for the wide grin he always seemed to have when playing for Liverpool.

SATURDAY 4th MARCH 2000

A sign of the times, perhaps, as Liverpool's starting XI against Premier League leaders Manchester United contains just two English players for the first time in the club's history. Jamie Carragher and Dominic Matteo are the sole representatives of England with Robbie Fowler, Steven Gerrard and Jamie Redknapp all unavailable on the day. The Reds still take a creditable point at Old Trafford in a 1-1 draw but remain ten points adrift of Sir Alex Ferguson's men as a result.

WEDNESDAY 4th MARCH 1981

A memorable night at Anfield as Liverpool destroy CSKA Sofia 5-1 in the European Cup third round, first leg. A Graeme Souness hat-trick and goals from Sammy Lee and Terry McDermott sandwiched in-between make the second leg in Bulgaria little more than a formality and the Reds' 1-0 win completes a 6-1 aggregate victory – and earns Bob Paisley's side a place in the semi-finals where Bayern Munich await.

SATURDAY 4th MARCH 1955

The Reds' porous defence sees their long unbeaten home record crumble against Stoke City. Having gone a dozen matches without losing at Anfield – winning the majority of them despite losing most of their away games – title-chasing Stoke prove too strong and though John Evans scores twice, the Potters leave Merseyside with a 4-2 win.

TUESDAY 5th MARCH 1996

Paul Stewart brings a close to a disappointing spell with Liverpool by joining Sunderland. The former Manchester City and Tottenham star joined the Reds for a fee of £2.3m three years earlier, but never came close to the form that made him one of English football's hottest properties at City. He spent just under four years at Anfield, but played only 42 games and managed just three goals during that time. Stewart struggled with injuries and was loaned out several times towards the end of his time on Merseyside which, for some fans and possibly the player himself, couldn't come quickly enough.

SATURDAY 6th MARCH 1948

Albert Stubbins scores all four goals as Liverpool thrash Huddersfield Town 4-0 at Anfield. The Reds' number nine opens the scoring after just three minutes and then adds a second on 19 minutes. He completes his quadruple with further strikes on 54 and 60 minutes in his one-man demolition of the Terriers. The win is one of eight in the last 11 games for the Reds, who went into this game in terrible form having lost five of their previous six and failed to score for 527 minutes! Stubbins scores 83 goals in 180 career appearances for the Reds during a seven-year stint.

SAMMY LEE — INDUSTRY MIXED WITH SKILL. TERRIFIC SERVANT FOR THE REDS (SEE 4TH MARCH 1981).

SUNDAY 6th MARCH 2011

Liverpool beat Manchester United after a stunning display at Anfield against the champions-elect. Kenny Dalglish's revitalised Reds take the league leaders apart with Luis Suarez magnificent and Dirk Kuyt deadly – the Dutchman's hat-trick giving the hosts a 3-0 lead before Javier Hernandez pulled a late consolation goal back for United. It was the Reds' third successive win over Sir Alex Ferguson's side at home, much to the delight of the sell-out Anfield crowd.

SATURDAY 7th MARCH 1964

Liverpool's title bid takes a major boost with a thumping 6-0 win over basement side Ipswich Town at Anfield. The Tractor Boys hold out for 41 minutes before Ian St John breaks the deadlock – and the floodgates opened. Roger Hunt makes it 2-0 three minutes after the break and Alf Arrowsmith scores the first of his brace seven minutes later. Peter Thompson bangs in number four after 70 minutes and Hunts adds a fifth two minutes later before Arrowsmith wraps up the scoring on 83 minutes.

WEDNESDAY 8th MARCH 1966

Liverpool progress to a second successive major European competition semi-final following a 2-0 victory over Honved. Chris Lawlor and Ian St John score the goals for the Reds who had arguably done the hard work in Hungary, holding Honved to a priceless 0-0 draw.

THURSDAY 9th MARCH 2001

Liverpool grind out a 0-0 draw away to Porto in the first leg of the Uefa Cup fifth round. It's a classic European rearguard by Gerard Houllier's men who will complete the job 2-0 at Anfield a week later.

FRIDAY 10th MARCH 2000

Emile Heskey joins Liverpool for a mammoth £11m fee from Leicester City. The 22-year-old striker scored 22 goals in 56 games in his first year at Anfield and the Reds won three trophies – things couldn't have gone better for the England striker. But this was as good as it got for Heskey and he rarely hit the heights of his first full season and he moved to Birmingham City in May 2004 having played 223 games, netting 60 times.

WEDNESDAY 11th MARCH 2008

Liverpool move into the Champions League quarter-finals after a superb 1-0 win over Inter Milan at the San Siro Stadium, silencing the 71,000-plus crowd in the process. Leading 2-0 from the first leg, Rafa Benitez's side were confident, focused and determined from the kick-off and when Fernando Torres scored the winner on 68 minutes, it was no more than the Reds deserved.

SATURDAY 12th MARCH 1921

Future Reds boss Joe Fagan is born. Fagan packed more into his brief spell as boss than most do in a career winning a hat-trick of trophies and making the Reds the kings of Europe and England in the process – not bad for one of the more modest Boot Room graduates. Not unlike Bob Paisley, he was a reluctant incumbent of the hot-seat, preferring to remain in the background and watch the club he loved win trophy after trophy. The hugely likeable Fagan – who had enjoyed the majority of his playing career with Manchester City – could have continued to be successful in his role, but just as the Boot Room boys before him who had taken the reins, when he felt he'd taken the club as far as he could, he stepped aside for the next man. For Joe, Liverpool FC always came first.

SATURDAY 12th MARCH 1955

Liverpool's dramatic turn of fortunes on the road continues with a third successive win at Bury. The Reds had lost 11 and drawn two of their Division Two games away from Anfield before recording victories at Fulham and Notts County. The game at Gigg Lane was all about one man – John Evans – with the Liverpool number ten netting after 16, 29, 47 and 70 minutes, though the Shakers battled until the end, ultimately going down 4-3.

SATURDAY 13th MARCH 1982

Two goals from Ronnie Whelan, and one from Ian Rush, help Liverpool retain the League Cup; the first team to do so since Nottingham Forest had beaten Liverpool, and then Southampton, in consecutive years in 1978 and 1979. Tottenham Hotspur were brushed aside as Liverpool won 3-1 at Wembley Stadium in their first League Cup Final since they beat Norwich City in 1973.

TUESDAY 14th MARCH 1995

Jan Molby's 42nd penalty for Liverpool is not enough to save the Reds on a miserable night at Anfield. Roy Evans' team are cut to shreds by a Peter Ndlovu hat-trick and Ron Atkinson's Coventry City in a 3-2 victory. Just over 27,000 fans turn out to see the defeat – and even David Burrows' injury-time consolation is barely merited by Evans' lacklustre team.

SATURDAY 14th MARCH 2009

A memorable day for all Liverpool fans as Rafa Benitez's side beat Manchester United 4-1 at Old Trafford. Despite falling behind to a 23rd-minute penalty from Cristiano Ronaldo, Fernando Torres levelled five minutes later and Steven Gerrard tucked home a penalty on 44 minutes to give the Reds a 2-1 lead at the break. As expected, United piled on the pressure in the second half, but Fabio Aurelio struck with a classic sucker punch on 77 minutes and Andrea Dossena put the icing on the cake with a fourth in stoppage time.

TUESDAY 15th MARCH 1892

Club owner John Houlding attempts to retain Everton FC after an acrimonious split with fellow board members and instead forms a new club – Liverpool – and after agreeing an amicable solution with the city's rugby team of the same name, one of the greatest football clubs in the world is born.

SATURDAY 15th MARCH 2008

Javier Mascherano scores his first Liverpool goal in a 2-1 victory over Reading at Anfield. The Argentine midfielder joins the Reds initially on loan before securing a permanent deal costing the club £18.6m from West Ham United. His goal – scored in the 19th minute – is one of only two scored during 139 appearances for the Reds over a three-year period before he leaves Merseyside for Barcelona.

SATURDAY 16th MARCH 2005

Lowly Blackburn Rovers grind out a 0-0 draw at Anfield and the Reds leave Anfield to a chorus of boos. The result is symptomatic of a disappointing campaign and despite there being a quarter of the season still to play, Liverpool are 30 points behind leaders Chelsea!

SATURDAY 17th MARCH 1973

A John Mahoney own goal on 65 minutes gives Bill Shankly's Liverpool a 1-0 win away to Stoke City at the Victoria Ground. The hard-fought victory means the Reds pull two points clear of second-place Arsenal who were involved in a sixth-round FA Cup tie the same day.

SUNDAY 18th MARCH 1990

John Barnes scores twice to give Liverpool a satisfying 2-1 win over Manchester United at Old Trafford. This was also a game when Ronnie Whelan scored an incredible 30-yard chipped own goal – regarded by many as the greatest own goal ever scored! The victory leaves the Reds two points adrift of leaders Aston Villa while United slip to within three points of the bottom three – happy days!

THURSDAY 18th MARCH 2010

Two Fernando Torres goals, and another from skipper Steve Gerrard, put the Reds into the Europa League quarter-finals following a 3-0 victory over Lille. The French side had won the first leg 1-0, but had no answer to the brilliance of Torres who struck in the 49th and 89th minutes after Gerrard's penalty had levelled aggregates just nine minutes into the game.

SATURDAY 19th MARCH 1980

Liverpool beat an ailing Leeds United side 3-0 at Anfield to move six points clear of second-place Manchester United. Alan Kennedy's goal is sandwiched between two David Johnson strikes in front of more than 37,000 fans. The Reds' home form is the key to lifting the title with 15 wins and six draws at Anfield and just eight goals conceded.

SATURDAY 20th MARCH 1988

Everton gain sweet revenge for the FA Cup defeat by Everton a month earlier by ending the Reds 29-match unbeaten run at Goodison Park – one of only two league defeats for Dalglish's squad in the 1987/88 season. Everton bring the run to an end through a goal from Wayne Clarke.

THURSDAY 20th MARCH 2003

Alan Thompson and John Hartson score a goal in each half to give Celtic a shock 2-0 win at Anfield in the Uefa Cup quarter-final second leg. Having drawn the first leg 1-1 at Parkhead, the Reds began as strong favourites in front of a sell-out crowd, but the Bhoys proved too strong on the night and it was they, not Liverpool, who progressed to the last four of the competition.

SUNDAY 20th MARCH 2005

For the first time in Liverpool's history, all three substitutions are made before half-time due to injuries sustained in a feisty Merseyside derby at Anfield. Steven Gerrard and Luis Garcia score a goal each in the space of five minutes in the period to see off Everton in front of a sell-out crowd. Tim Cahill's 75th-minute goal set up a grandstand finish during which the Reds had two walking wounded who were unable to be replaced.

TUESDAY 21st MARCH 2006

Liverpool produce a stunning display away to Birmingham City, winning 7-0 at a stunned St Andrew's to move into the semi-finals of the FA Cup. The Reds never look back after Sami Hyypia's first-minute goal and Peter Crouch makes it 2-0 on six minutes. Crouch adds another before half-time and further strikes from Fernando Morientes, John Arne Riise, an own goal by Olivier Tebily and a last-minute effort from Djibril Cisse give Rafa Benitez his biggest win as Liverpool manager. All FA Cup quarter-finals were played in midweek for the first time due to England's involvement in the World Cup.

WEDNESDAY 22nd MARCH 1978

Nottingham Forest win the League Cup for the first time after John Robertson scored the only goal from the penalty spot in a replay at Old Trafford, after the initial tie had finished 0-0 at Wembley Stadium. There was much debate about the penalty, after television replays showed that Phil Thompson's challenge on John O'Hare was outside the penalty area, but referee Pat Partridge pointed to the spot and it was enough to see Liverpool's first League Cup Final appearance end in defeat.

LUIS GARCIA SCORES AGAINST EVERTON IN A FULL-BLOODED MERSEYSIDE DERBY (SEE 20TH MARCH 2005).

SATURDAY 22nd MARCH 1986

Liverpool beat Oxford United 6-0 at Anfield with Ian Rush and Jan Molby both scoring two goals. Mark Lawrenson and Ronnie Whelan are also on target in the romp. Oxford had proved plucky opponents earlier in the season, holding the Reds to a 2-2 draw at a packed Manor Ground. Liverpool are once again imperious on their own patch during the 1985/86 campaign, winning 16 times and drawing four on their way to yet another title.

SATURDAY 23rd MARCH 1991

Liverpool thrash Derby County 7-1 at the Baseball Ground. John Barnes, Ian Rush and Jan Molby score before the break and Barnes, Steve Nicol (2) and Ray Houghton complete the rout in the second period.

SATURDAY 24th MARCH 1934

Liverpool hover precariously above the Division One drop zone after a crushing 5-1 defeat by Leeds United at Elland Road. Fewer than 13,000 turn out for the game and Gordon Hodgson's solitary reply is the only crumb of comfort Reds' fans take back to Merseyside with them. The loss leaves Liverpool two points above second-bottom Sheffield United.

SATURDAY 25th MARCH 1908

Anfield bears witness to an incredible game as Liverpool beat league leaders Manchester United 7-4. In a see-saw encounter watched by just 10,000 fans, the Reds' scorers are Joe Hewitt (2), Bill McPherson (3) and Robbie Robinson (2) – it's one of the first of many epic encounters between the two north-west giants.

SATURDAY 26th MARCH 1983

Ronnie Whelan scores the winning goal in extra time as Liverpool beat Manchester United 2-1 after extra time to win the League Cup for the third successive season. Norman Whiteside had given United the lead after just 12 minutes, but with just 15 minutes of normal time left to play Alan Kennedy – who had scored so many crucial goals before – popped up with another to send the tie to extra time. Whelan ensured manager Bob Paisley would win his last major final in charge of the club.

SATURDAY 27th MARCH 1982

Craig Johnston rounds off a fantastic Liverpool performance as Bob Paisley's team run out 3-1 winners against Everton at Goodison Park. The club were flying high at the top of Division One, and goals were easy to come by. Ronnie Whelan got Liverpool's first when he bagged his 11th goal of the campaign midway through the first half. Scottish midfield maestro Graeme Souness added a second with his sixth of the season just before the hour mark before Johnston scored only his second goal for the club with nine minutes left to round off a terrific derby win.

SATURDAY 28th MARCH 1962

The red-hot Reds' goalscoring streak continues as Liverpool make it 27 goals in nine games with a 4-1 win over Preston North End in front of almost 40,000 Anfield fans. Jimmy Melia opens the scoring after nine minutes and Ian St John makes it 2-0 on 14. Roger Hunt completes the rout with goals after 37 and 67 minutes as Bill Shankly's era really begins to take effect. Liverpool go on to win the title and return to the top flight for the first time in nine years – and never look back.

WEDNESDAY 28th MARCH 1984

Liverpool retain the League Cup following a 1-0 win over Everton in a replay at Maine Road, with the only goal coming in the first half through Graeme Souness. The initial tie was uneventful and ended 0-0 at Wembley Stadium on March 25th. However, the game was overshadowed by the referee's decision not to award the Toffees a penalty when Alan Hansen appeared to divert Graeme Sharp's shot off the line.

MONDAY 29th MARCH 1937

Gordon Milne is born in Preston, England. The sturdy half-back was part of two championship-winning sides during his seven years at Anfield between 1960 and 1967. The England international, capped 14 times by his country, made 282 appearances – starting every game but two, both in his final campaign at the club. Milne left Liverpool at the age of 30, having contributed 18 goals in his tenure. A fine return for a fantastic servant of the club.

TUESDAY 30th MARCH 1976

John Toshack scores the only goal of the game as Liverpool win their Uefa Cup semi-final first leg against Barcelona at the Nou Camp. It was the Welsh striker's 21st goal of the season, and one of his most important as it gave the club an away goal going into the home leg. Toshack had previously scored three hat-tricks before this game – against Hibernian, Birmingham City and West Ham United – and his 16 league goals were a major contribution as Liverpool went on to win the Uefa Cup and the Division One title.

TUESDAY 30th MARCH 1982

Two goals from Ian Rush and another from Terry McDermott give Liverpool a fourth successive league win after seeing off Birmingham City 3-1 at Anfield. It's one of eleven wins on the bounce for the Reds who go on to win the title in a canter – this after a disappointing fifth-place finish the previous season.

MONDAY 31st MARCH 1975

Stoke City inflict a mortal blow on the Reds' title hopes with a 2-0 win at the Victoria Ground in one of the tightest championships ever.

SATURDAY 31st MARCH 1984

John Wark scores a debut goal as Liverpool beat Watford 2-0 at Vicarage Road in a Division One clash. The midfielder opens the scoring just before the hour mark and Ian Rush adds a second with ten minutes left to play. Wark joined Liverpool from Ipswich Town after scoring 136 goals in 384 appearances and during his time at Anfield he scored 42 goals and, ironically, he scored his 100th league goal in a home game against Ipswich Town on 24th November 1984.

SATURDAY 31st MARCH 1986

Steve McMahon scores a goal in each half as Liverpool ease past Manchester City 2-0 at Anfield. It's payback for the league leaders who surprisingly lost 1-0 at Maine Road on Boxing Day and the start of seven successive victories that ensure the Division One title returns to Anfield after a year away.

LIVERPOOL FC
On This Day

APRIL

WEDNESDAY 1st APRIL 1981

Liverpool win the League Cup for the first time after beating West Ham United in a replay at Villa Park. The initial game had finished 1-1 at Wembley Stadium, with Ray Stewart equalising from the penalty spot for the Hammers after Alan Kennedy had given Liverpool the lead. West Ham took the lead in the replay through Paul Goddard, but goals from Kenny Dalglish and Alan Hansen complete the comeback to ensure the first League Cup triumph for the Reds.

SATURDAY 2nd APRIL 1955

Alex South scores his first goal for Liverpool in his fifth game for the club during a 4-4 draw with Luton Town at Anfield. The defender only makes seven appearances for the club before joining Halifax Town, where he excels in the somewhat modest surrounds of West Yorkshire. South had only recently signed from Brighton & Hove Albion in December 1954, but failed to force his way into the first team. John Evans scored twice either side of an Eric Anderson goal before South added a fourth, which proved to be his first and last!

MONDAY 3rd APRIL 1972

Phil Thompson makes his debut as Liverpool stroll to a 3-0 victory over Manchester United at Old Trafford. The Liverpool-born and bred defender came on as a substitute for the scorer of the second goal, John Toshack, with nine minutes left to play. It was Thompson's only appearance of the season, but he would go on to play a crucial role over the next decade as he became one of the most decorated footballers in the history of English football, winning a host of major honours – including seven league titles and two European Cups.

SATURDAY 4th APRIL 1908

Diminutive inside forward Ronald Orr scores Liverpool's only goal on his debut as Tom Watson's team are brushed aside emphatically by Aston Villa in Birmingham. The match ended 5-1 but was the start of a decent spell for Orr, who arrived at the club from Newcastle United for the princely sum of £350. The Scotsman went on to make 112 appearances for Liverpool over three years, scoring 39 goals in the process.

SUNDAY 5th APRIL 1987

Charlie Nicholas scores twice as Arsenal beat Liverpool 2-1 in the League Cup Final at Wembley Stadium. Ian Rush had given Liverpool the lead on 23 minutes, but just seven minutes later former Celtic star Nicholas had pulled the Gunners level before netting the winner with seven minutes to go. It was the first time the Reds had lost in the final since 1978, when Nottingham Forest won in a replay.

SUNDAY 5th APRIL 1995

Two goals from Steve McManaman are enough to win the League Cup for Liverpool, as Roy Evans claims his first major silverware in charge of the club. Liverpool academy graduate McManaman was named as Man of the Match after his scintillating performance, and the game was even dubbed the 'McManaman Final' by some fans. Alan Thompson scored a sensational goal for Bolton Wanderers, but it was not enough as the Reds ran out 2-1 winners to lift the trophy for the fifth time.

WEDNESDAY 6th APRIL 1977

Liverpool beat FC Zurich 3-1 in their European Cup semi-final first leg at the Letzigrund Stadium to give themselves a huge advantage going into the home tie. Phil Neal scores twice, one a penalty, either side of a Steve Heighway goal, in Switzerland to all-but seal the club's progress to the final of Europe's top competition. Liverpool won the tournament following a 3-2 victory over Borussia Monchengladbach in Rome on May 25th.

SATURDAY 7th APRIL 2007

Alvaro Arbeloa scores his first goal for Liverpool in a 2-1 win over Reading at the Madejski Stadium. The Spaniard had been at the club for three months following his £2.64m transfer from Deportivo La Coruna, and scored the opening goal of the game after 15 minutes. Dirk Kuyt added a second – the winner – with five minutes left, after coming off the bench in the second half. Arbeloa made 98 appearances for the club before joining Real Madrid for around £3.5m; he scored only one more goal before his departure – the last in a 3-0 win over West Bromwich Albion at Anfield. Robbie Keane scored the other two.

SATURDAY 8th APRIL 1978

Energetic midfielder Sammy Lee scores a debut goal as Liverpool beat Leicester City 3-2 in a thrilling encounter at Anfield. Lee replaced the injured David Johnson after just six minutes after he tore his knee ligaments – and what an impact the 17-year-old made. His goal, sandwiched in between strikes from Tommy Smith, was the first of 19 for the club in 295 games over nine years. During his time at Liverpool he won three league titles and two European Cups. Lee would return in later years to become first-team coach at Anfield.

WEDNESDAY 8th APRIL 2008

Following a 1-1 first-leg draw at the Emirates Stadium, Liverpool set up another Champions League semi-final clash with Chelsea after a breathtaking game at Anfield – though the Reds left it late. Fernando Torres puts Rafa Benitez's side 2-1 up after Abou Diaby and Sami Hyypia's earlier strikes, but Emmanuel Adebayor stunned Anfield when he levelled for the Gunners with six minutes left to play. The visitors were seemingly on their way through via the away goals rule – but the drama wasn't over. Liverpool immediately went up the other end and won a penalty, which was calmly dispatched by Steven Gerrard, before Ryan Babel put the result beyond doubt at the death to send Anfield wild – and the Reds into the semis.

WEDNESDAY 9th APRIL 1975

Robert 'Robbie' Bernard Fowler is born in Toxeth, Liverpool. Few realised in his formative years that the skinny youngster would go on to become one of the world's most feared strikers. Although he is one of the greatest players in Liverpool's history, he was at the club at a time when trophies were few and far between, and, although he won two FA Cups and two League Cups, he never got his hands on the most coveted prize in English domestic football – the Premier League title. He played 369 times for Liverpool, and scored 183 goals, in two spells with the club before making his final farewell and joining Championship side Cardiff City in July 2007.

FRIDAY 10th APRIL 1936

Matt Busby scores his first goal for Liverpool in a 2-2 draw with Blackburn Rovers just one month after signing from Manchester City. Costing the Reds £8,000, the Scottish half-back, who appeared for his country seven times during the war, scored Liverpool's first of the game just two minutes after the interval, with Fred Howe netting the other. Busby made his debut in a 1-0 defeat to Huddersfield Town at Leeds Road on March 14th 1936 before making a further 121 appearances, scoring three goals in total. It's somewhat ironic that the man who made Manchester United a world force in years to come actually plied his trade for United's two greatest rivals in City and Liverpool – without ever playing for the Old Trafford side.

MONDAY 11th APRIL 2011

Andy Carroll opens his Liverpool goalscoring account with a double against big spending Manchester City at Anfield. His first goal 13 minutes into the game beats City goalkeeper Joe Hart from long range before he completes the scoring in a 3-0 win with a close-range header ten minutes before half-time. Dirk Kuyt got the second just a minute earlier. The game also saw a first appearance for 18-year-old Jon Flanagan, who deputised at right-back.

SATURDAY 12th APRIL 1969

Emlyn Hughes scores his third goal of the season, and Ian Callaghan bags what proves to be the winner, as the Reds beat Leicester City 2-1 at Filbert Street to keep their title hopes alive. Though trailing leaders Leeds by five points, Bill Shankly's team have a game in hand and a game against the Lilywhites still to come.

SATURDAY 12th APRIL 1986

Ronnie Whelan scores a hat-trick as Liverpool thrash Coventry City 5-0 at Anfield. Whelan scored twice in six first-half minutes to put his side 2-0 up before Jan Molby and Ian Rush put the game beyond doubt with second-half goals. Whelan completes the scoring, and his hat-trick, in the 83rd minute to keep the club on course for its 16th Division One title.

MONDAY 13th APRIL 1998

Local lad David Thompson gets his first-ever Liverpool goal nearly two years after bursting onto the scene as an 18-year-old. After coming on as a substitute for Danny Murphy with a little over 15 minutes to play, the former England under-21 international scores the winner in a 2-1 victory over Crystal Palace in front of a jubilant Anfield crowd. Thompson scored another four goals before joining Coventry City in the summer of 2000.

SATURDAY 14th APRIL 1906

Reds boss Tom Watson wins his second Division One title as Liverpool win 2-0 against already-relegated Wolverhampton Wanderers at Molineux. The club were already one point clear of Preston North End, but the Lilywhites were comfortably beaten 3-0 by Stoke City at the Victoria Ground, ensuring the league title would be heading to Anfield for a second time. Liverpool ended the season with a 3-1 win over Sheffield United in front of a celebratory home crowd.

SATURDAY 14th APRIL 1973

Kevin Keegan tucks away a penalty on 14 minutes for his 11th goal of the season. It proves to be the only goal of the game in a 1-0 win over West Bromwich Albion as the Reds power their way towards a first title for seven years.

WEDNESDAY 14th APRIL 2009

On the 20th anniversary of Hillsborough, Liverpool come close to one of the most amazing comebacks in Champions League history as Rafa Benitez's side attempt to overturn a 3-1 first-leg defeat. With a place in the semi-final awaiting the winners, the Reds race into a 2-0 half-time lead thanks to goals from Fabio Aurelio and Xabi Alonso. Second-half goals from Didier Drogba, Alex and Frank Lampard restored Chelsea's control of the tie and gave the hosts a 6-3 lead on aggregate, but Liverpool weren't finished and Lucas and Dirk Kuyt scored in quick succession to make it 4-3 with less than ten minutes left, but Lampard scored a late fourth on the break to make it 4-4 and send Benitez's brave side out.

FERNANDO TORRES BATTLES TO HELP LIVERPOOL ACHIEVE MISSION IMPOSSIBLE (SEE 14TH APRIL 2009).

SATURDAY 15th APRIL 1989

Disaster strikes at Hillsborough as 96 people tragically lose their lives after being crushed to death while standing on the terraces. The day was supposed to be one of the greatest spectacles of the football season, as two giants of the English game met to compete an FA Cup semi-final tie, but nobody could have predicted the horrors that would unfold. Nottingham Forest were given the Spion Kop End of Hillsborough, which could hold 21,000 fans, whereas Liverpool supporters had nearly 7,000 less tickets allocated in the Leppings Lane End. As kick-off approached, the police allowed thousands of fans into the ground to avoid crushing outside the stadium, but once people continued to flood down the middle tunnel into the centre pens, unaware of the effect it was having on those at the front of the terrace, English football suffered its greatest ever tragedy. Uninjured fans tore down advertising boards to use as stretchers in order to help in any way they could after escaping by climbing over the fence to safety before a gate was eventually opened. Amongst the victims was Jon-Paul Gilhooley, cousin of Liverpool and England midfielder Steven Gerrard.

MONDAY 15th APRIL 1991

Ronnie Moran steps down as caretaker manager following a thrilling 5-4 victory over Leeds United at Elland Road. He only spent ten games in charge of Liverpool, losing five but winning four – one of which was an emphatic 7-1 thumping of Derby County at the Baseball Ground. His form as Liverpool manager saw the club slip from a commanding position at the top of the table, conceding ground on eventual winners Arsenal.

SATURDAY 16th APRIL 1966

Liverpool win the Division One title for the seventh time after beating Stoke City 2-0 at Anfield. Geoff Strong and Ian St John score the goals in front of an ecstatic 41,106 crowd. With three games of the season left, Bill Shankly's team had built an unassailable lead at the top of the league, despite Leeds United beating Everton 4-1 at Elland Road. Liverpool went on to win one, draw one and lose one of their remaining league games.

WEDNESDAY 16th APRIL 1974

Liverpool destroy Manchester City in the first 35 minutes of a vital clash at Anfield. With the Reds chasing leaders Leeds United in a bid to retain the Division One title, two goals from Brian Hall and another from Phil Boersma give the hosts a 3-0 lead with just 16 minutes on the clock and when Kevin Keegan adds a fourth on 35 minutes, the game is effectively over. Despite leading 4-0 at the break, there's no further scoring in the second half.

MONDAY 17th APRIL 1922

With three games still left to play, David Ashworth guides his side to a 2-1 victory over Burnley to ensure Liverpool are crowned champions of England for the third time. Ashworth is aided by his former club Oldham Athletic, who beat second-place Tottenham Hotspur 1-0 at Boundary Park, giving Liverpool an unassailable lead at the top of Division One. Liverpool went on to lose two of the games, but it did not matter in the end.

SATURDAY 17th APRIL 1982

Kenny Dalglish scores the winning goal against West Bromwich Albion in a tense match at Anfield. The 71st-minute strike from Dalglish is the Reds' ninth consecutive victory and puts Liverpool on the verge of yet another league title and five points clear of second-placed Ipswich Town.

SATURDAY 18th APRIL 1964

Bill Shankly wins his first English championship as Liverpool manager with three games to spare, as the club finish four points clear of Manchester United to claim a sixth league title, following a 5-0 victory over Arsenal at Anfield. Liverpool were already in a commanding position at the top of the table after beating United 3-0 on April 4th at Anfield.

SATURDAY 18th APRIL 1981

A disappointing campaign edges closer to its conclusion with a dour 0-0 draw with Leeds United at Elland Road. The Reds, 11 points behind leaders Aston Villa, meekly surrender the title and limp to a fifth-place finish.

MONDAY 19th APRIL 1976

Liverpool win 3-0 against Manchester City at Maine Road to move three points clear of Queens Park Rangers and ensure the title is returning to Anfield for a ninth time – the first time under manager Bob Paisley. Despite QPR's efforts, their 2-1 win against Arsenal at Loftus Road was not enough, and a final-day-of-the-season win over Leeds United rounds off a successful season for the London club.

TUESDAY 19th APRIL 1983

Despite Liverpool failing to win in their last seven games, they are crowned champions of England for the second consecutive season and for the 14th time in their history. It would be the last season that Bob Paisley is in charge of the club, and he finished the campaign 11 points clear of Watford, who won 2-1 at Anfield on the final day of the campaign. The alarming slump in form is a concern for incoming boss Joe Fagan.

WEDNESDAY 20th APRIL 1935

Liverpool follow up a 5-0 win over Stoke City with a 6-0 victory over Chelsea as the Reds' rich end-of-season form continues. Two goals from Vic Wright – plus another two from Berry Nieuwenhuys – and one each from Lance Carr and Fred Howe complete the rout.

MONDAY 20th APRIL 1992

A forgettable evening at Highbury as Arsenal blast four past the Reds on a torrid visit to north London. It was the last season before the Premier League's introduction and the Gunners couldn't stop scoring at home having won their previous game 4-1 against Crystal Palace. David Hillier put the Gunners in front and Ian Wright scored twice either side of Anders Limpar's brilliant chip from just over the halfway line.

SATURDAY 20th APRIL 1974

Everton all-but end the Reds' hopes of winning the title with a gritty 0-0 draw at Anfield. Going into the game, Liverpool trailed leaders Leeds United by four points – but with two games in hand. With Leeds winning, the Reds are forced to accept the title is heading back to Elland Road.

SATURDAY 21st APRIL 1923

With Sunderland losing 2-0 against Burnley at Turf Moor, and Liverpool earning a point at home against the previous season's FA Cup and Charity Shield winners Huddersfield Town, it was confirmed that Matt McQueen's side would win the Division One title for the second consecutive season. After the resignation of David Ashworth earlier in the campaign, the club had a poor run of form towards the end of the season, but the lead at the top of the table built by Ashworth proved to be enough in the end.

MONDAY 21st APRIL 2009

An epic eight-goal thriller as Liverpool and Arsenal produce a classic Monday night feast for the watching millions on Sky Sports. Despite the final score of 4-4, Arsenal led at half-time by just a goal to nil, courtesy of Andrei Arshavin, who added three more after the interval. Fernando Torres and Yossi Benayoun both scored twice for the Reds in a see-saw match, but ultimately it was two points dropped for Rafa Benitez's side who still went top of the Premier League ahead of Manchester United on goal difference with the point they gained.

FRIDAY 21st APRIL 2000

Controversies abound in the 162nd Merseyside derby as Everton keep the Reds at bay in a fiery 0-0 draw at Goodison Park. Though Liverpool know there is no way they can overhaul leaders Manchester United, Champions League football was yet to be guaranteed so a point was a reasonable result, but it seemed as though the Toffees had pinched the points in injury time as Don Hutchison blocked a Sander Westerveld clearance and as the ball rolled towards the empty net, Graham Poll blew for full-time. The referee disallowed the goal, saying the match was over, much to the chagrin of the home players and fans.

WEDNESDAY 22nd APRIL 1981

Ray Kennedy's 83rd-minute goal is enough to earn Liverpool a 1-1 draw in the second leg of the European Cup semi-final away to Bayern Munich. After a 0-0 draw at Anfield, the Germans seemed to have the advantage but Kennedy's goal sent the travelling Reds wild and his team through to the final on the away goals rule.

SATURDAY 23rd APRIL 2011

The Kenny Dalglish factor is still going strong as the Reds thrash Birmingham City 5-0. Maxi Rodriguez scores a hat-trick, Dirk Kuyt grabs one while Joe Cole's late fifth completes a memorable day at Anfield and serves a warning to the rest of the Premier League that Liverpool are becoming a force once again.

SATURDAY 24th APRIL 1979

David Johnson's goal on 12 minutes isn't enough to beat Southampton at The Dell as the Reds drop vital points. The 1-1 draw keeps Liverpool seven points clear of West Bromwich Albion and needing six points to seal yet another title.

SATURDAY 25th APRIL 1914

Ex-Everton forward Bert Freeman scores the only goal as Burnley win the FA Cup in the Reds' first final – and the last to be played at The Crystal Palace. It was the first final to be played in front a reigning monarch who, at the time, was George V. It would prove to be manager Tom Watson's first and last major final with Liverpool and he died in May 1915.

SATURDAY 25th APRIL 1978

Club legend Tommy Smith plays his last game for the club during a 1-0 win over Arsenal at Anfield. Smith, who was a former groundsman and trainee, went on to skipper the Reds and played 638 games and scored 48 goals in his illustrious career. Tough-tackling and uncompromising, Smith was one of the game's true hard men and he was committed to the Reds from his first game to the last. Few players have worn the shirt of Liverpool Football Club with more pride than Tommy Smith.

SATURDAY 26th APRIL 1986

Liverpool record their ninth win in ten games as the Reds hit peak form at the perfect time. Birmingham City are swept aside at Anfield and defender Gary Gillespie has a day he'll never forget as he bags a hat-trick in the 5-0 win. Ian Rush and Jan Molby also score but Molby hands over penalty-taking duties seven minutes from time so Gillespie can complete his treble.

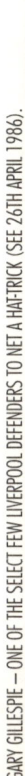

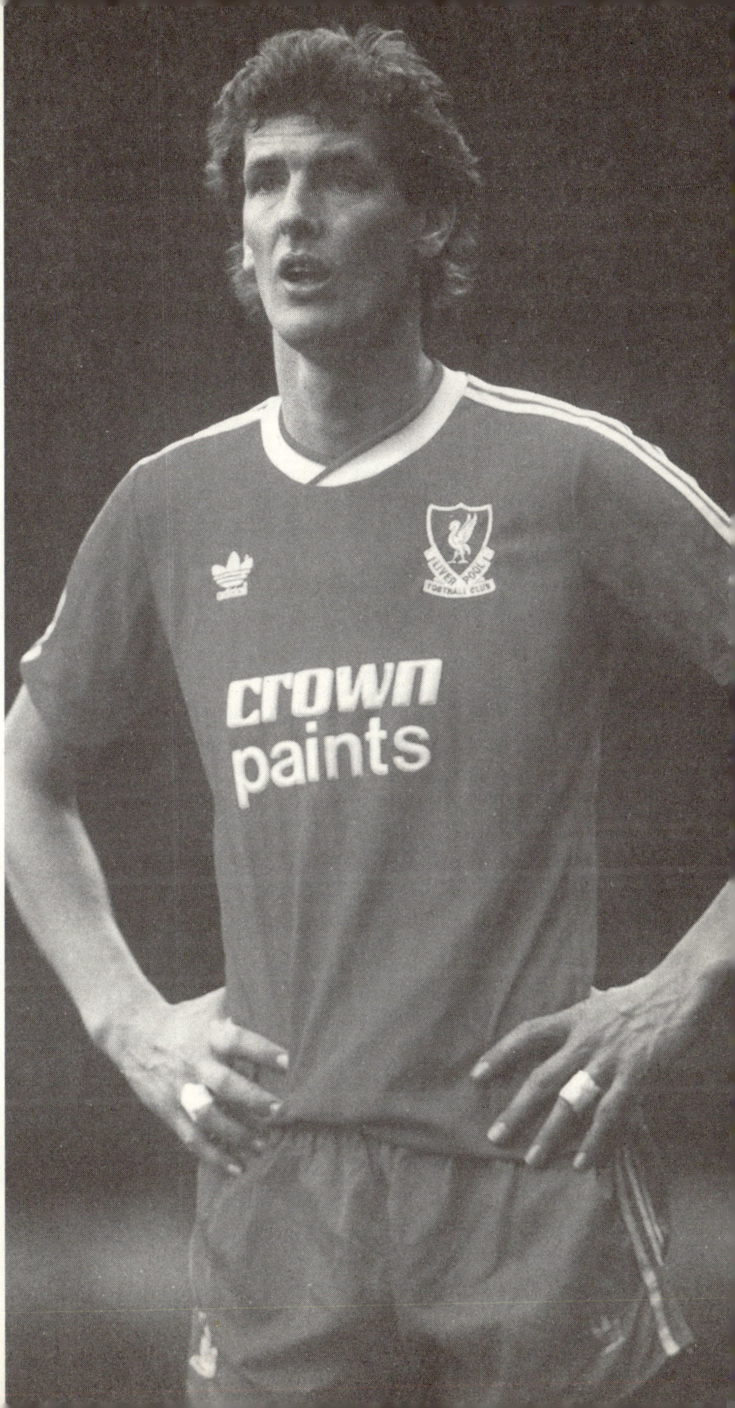

GARY GILLESPIE – ONE OF THE SELECT FEW LIVERPOOL DEFENDERS TO NET A HAT-TRICK (SEE 26TH APRIL 1986).

SATURDAY 27th APRIL 1991

Former Liverpool and Arsenal midfielder Ray Kennedy has a testimonial to remember as the Reds win 3-1 at Highbury. The Englishman won every domestic honour in the game during his time at Anfield, and repeated several of his achievements with the Gunners. He won 17 caps for his country and scored three times. Peter Beardsley, Jan Molby and David Speedie scored Liverpool's goals, and Kenny Dalglish made an appearance just months after resigning as manager.

SATURDAY 28th APRIL 1973

Liverpool claim their eighth Division One title following a 0-0 draw with Leicester City at Anfield, to move three points clear of Arsenal. The Gunners only had one game in hand – a tricky tie against Leeds United at Elland Road. The London side would go on to lose their remaining game emphatically, with Leeds winning 6-1. The game was irrelevant, however, as Liverpool had already been crowned champions of England for what would be Bill Shankly's last time.

WEDNESDAY 28th APRIL 1976

Bob Paisley's Liverpool are seemingly heading for defeat after falling 2-0 behind to FC Bruges at half-time in the first leg of the Uefa Cup Final at Anfield. Almost 50,000 home fans know that, barring a second-half miracle, there can be no way back with the Belgians already having two away goals in the bag. But, in one of the most remarkable five minutes ever witnessed at Liverpool's world famous home, Ray Kennedy, Jimmy Case and a Kevin Keegan penalty turn the game on its head with goals in the 59th, 61st and 64th minutes. With no further scoring, Bruges still start the second leg as favourites for the Uefa Cup, knowing a 1-0 win will be enough...

SATURDAY 28th APRIL 1990

Liverpool beat Queens Park Rangers 2-1 to seal their 18th Division One title with two games left to play. It had been nip and tuck for the majority of the season between the Reds and Aston Villa, who had moved to within two points with four games to go. But Liverpool won all of their remaining games to finish nine points clear of the Villains.

MONDAY 29th APRIL 1901

Liverpool win the Division One title for the first time after beating West Bromwich Albion 1-0 at The Hawthorns on the final game of the season. Tom Watson guided the club to its first major silverware, finishing the season two points ahead of Sunderland who were top of the league before kick-off, having won 2-0 against Newcastle United at St James' Park just five days earlier.

SATURDAY 29th APRIL 1950

Reg Lewis scores twice as Arsenal beat Liverpool 2-0 in the FA Cup Final at Wembley Stadium. The goals came either side of half-time in a game which is remembered for the controversial decision made by George Kay to leave out defender Bob Paisley, who had scored in the 2-0 semi-final win over Everton at Anfield in March. Paisley would, of course, return to Wembley many times in the future – as Liverpool manager – perhaps driven by events of that day.

WEDNESDAY 29th APRIL 1992

A little over 4,000 people turn up to watch Wayne Harrison's testimonial match between Oldham Athletic and Liverpool at Boundary Park. Although the midfielder played for neither club, he began his career at Everton before flitting in and out of non-league football. He had spells with Sheffield Wednesday, Blackpool and Burnley during the 1970s and 1980s before ending his career at Finnish outfit Oulun Palloseura. Don Hutchinson and Ronny Rosenthal scored the goals for Liverpool, as the game finished 2-2.

SATURDAY 30th APRIL 1977

The Division One title is all-but decided on a dramatic day in the race for the championship. Liverpool knew they needed to beat third-place Ipswich Town and hope relegation-haunted Derby County could beat second-place Manchester City. Late goals from Ray Kennedy and Kevin Keegan helped the Reds win 2-1 against Bobby Robson's talented outfit while City were thrashed 4-0 at the Baseball Ground – it was a dream day for Liverpool fans, but a disaster for the Blues who chose the worst time possible for an off day. Liverpool went on to win the title by a single point after failing to win the final four games.

SATURDAY 30th APRIL 1986

Ian Rush and Ronnie Whelan score the goals that mean Liverpool need one more win to win the league title. The 2-0 victory over Leicester City at Filbert Street means the Reds are four points clear of their nearest challengers West Ham United, with just one game to play. It's a sixth successive win and the blip the Hammers had been hoping for in order to make ground never materialised. Kenny Dalglish scores the winner in the final-day victory over Chelsea to ensure the title returns to Anfield.

SATURDAY 30th APRIL 1988

Liverpool draw 1-1 at Stamford Bridge to build an unassailable lead at the top of Division One and win the English championship for the 17th time. Kenny Dalglish's side were 15 points clear of Manchester United, who had won 2-1 at Old Trafford against Queens Park Rangers, but there were only three more games left to play of the season. In the end, United closed the gap to nine points, but the margin was still a significant one.

SATURDAY 30th APRIL 1994

A season that Liverpool fans can't wait to end – for reasons illustrated in this 1-0 home defeat to Norwich City. The Canaries, one of the best teams on the road during the 1993/94 season, record this famous Anfield win to draw within eight points of the Reds who have one more game to play.

WEDNESDAY 30th APRIL 2008

Liverpool see the chance to appear in another Champions League final taken away by Chelsea at Stamford Bridge. Having drawn 1-1 at Anfield, it was always going to be a big ask for Rafa Benitez's side and when Didier Drogba put the Blues 1-0 up on 33 minutes, the task became even greater. Fernando Torres had other ideas, however, equalising in the 64th minute and forcing the game into extra time. The Reds couldn't find a way past the home defence and goals from Frank Lampard and Drogba made it 3-1 before a Ryan Babel strike three minutes from the end gave the Reds some hope.

LIVERPOOL FC
On This Day

MAY

SATURDAY 1st MAY 1965

Ian St John scores the winner as Liverpool beat Leeds United 2-1 after extra time – the first FA Cup Final to go to extra time since 1947. Roger Hunt had given Liverpool the lead three minutes into the additional 30 before Billy Bremner equalised for the Yorkshire club. Hunt's goal was set up by left-back Gerry Byrne, who played the majority of the game with a broken collarbone.

SATURDAY 2nd MAY 1981

Sunderland record a rare away win at Anfield with a 1-0 victory – a second successive home reverse having lost by the same score to Manchester United in the previous Anfield match. The defeat means the Reds have now failed to win in five games.

SATURDAY 3rd MAY 1967

Willie Stevenson's 23rd-minute penalty against Leeds United at Elland Road is, remarkably, Liverpool's first first-half goal for ten games. Nine of the previous matches had been 0-0 at the break, but the celebrations were relatively short-lived as the Lilywhites recover to win 2-1.

SATURDAY 3rd MAY 1986

Liverpool win 1-0 against Chelsea at Stamford Bridge to stay five points clear of second-place Everton, who had won 6-1 against Southampton at Goodison Park, to win a 16th Division One title. The Toffees finished the season two points adrift after they won their final game 3-1 at home to West Ham United two days later. It was manager Kenny Dalglish's first major trophy as Liverpool boss, carrying on a fine tradition set by Bill Shankly, Bob Paisley and Joe Fagan.

TUESDAY 3rd MAY 2005

Luis Garcia's goal on four minutes against Chelsea sends the Reds into the European Cup Final for the first time in 20 years, though the victory wasn't without controversy. Milan Baros beat Petr Cech to the ball in a goalmouth scramble and Garcia tapped the ball home, despite Chelsea claiming it did not cross the line. The Reds' defence does the rest as they withstand everything Chelsea's largely ineffective attack could throw at them.

FRIDAY 4th MAY 1956

Don Welsh becomes the first manager to be sacked by Liverpool, having failed to restore the club's top-flight status after suffering relegation in 1954 – the first time the Reds had been out of Division One in 50 years. In the 1955/56 season, Welsh almost guided Liverpool back to the top tier of English football but his side just missed out on promotion, finishing four points adrift of Leeds United who finished second. Statistically, Welsh has the worst win percentage of any Liverpool manager.

SATURDAY 4th MAY 1974

Two second-half goals from Kevin Keegan, either side of a goal from Steve Heighway, make sure that Liverpool comfortably beat Newcastle United 3-0 in the FA Cup Final at Wembley. The game would be Bill Shankly's last in charge of the club as he later retired to spend more time with his family. Liverpool had beaten Leicester City and Ipswich Town, among others, en route to the final.

WEDNESDAY 5th MAY 1966

The Reds reach their first major European final, but the night ends in disappointment. More than 130,000 watch Liverpool beat Celtic 2-1 over two semi-finals, Reinhard Libuda scores the winner with ten minutes of extra time left to play as Borussia Dortmund beat Liverpool 2-1 to win the European Cup Winners' Cup at Hampden Park. Siegfried Held had given the Deutscher Fußballbund Cup (German Cup, or DFB Cup) winners the lead just after the hour mark, only for Roger Hunt to equalise for Liverpool five minutes later. With the game looking like it was going to penalties, Libuda struck to the dismay of the majority of the 41,657 crowd.

WEDNESDAY 5th MAY 1979

Bob Paisley claims his third Division One title with Liverpool as the club win the league for an 11th time. Liverpool beat Southampton 2-0 at Anfield to build an unassailable lead ahead of soon-to-be European champions Nottingham Forest at the top of the table with three games to go. Ultimately, Paisley's men finish eight points clear of Brian Clough's side after winning their remaining fixtures against Aston Villa, Middlesbrough and Leeds United.

THURSDAY 6th MAY 1915

After nearly 19 years at the helm, Liverpool boss Tom Watson dies aged 59 – just a fortnight after leading Liverpool to 14th place in Division One and to the club's first FA Cup Final, which was won 1-0 by Burnley. Having won the Second Division title in 1904/05, Watson then led the club to its second Division One title the following season. Watson had previously won the top-flight trophy in the 1900/01 campaign. He is Liverpool's longest-serving manager to date.

TUESDAY 6th MAY 1980

Bob Paisley wins yet another English championship, this time ahead of Manchester United, who finished two points behind his side. It is fitting that record-holders Liverpool should win the Division One title in its 100th competitive season. Even had the Red Devils won their final game of the season against Leeds United (which they lost 2-0 at Elland Road), Liverpool's superior goal difference meant that, barring two freak defeats, the title was always destined for Anfield for a 12th time.

SATURDAY 6th MAY 1997

Michael Owen becomes the club's youngest scorer when he scores just 16 minutes into his Liverpool debut. Aged 17 years and 144 days, Owen's historic goal couldn't prevent Wimbledon winning 2-1 at Selhurst Park.

SATURDAY 7th MAY 1988

Peter Beardsley and Craig Johnston both score twice as Liverpool thrash Sheffield Wednesday 5-1 at Hillsborough. Aussie midfielder Johnston opens the scoring on 31 minutes and John Barnes scores the second five minutes later. With the score 2-1 and just three minutes left, Beardsley scores twice in a minute before Johnston rounds the match off with a late fifth.

SUNDAY 8th MAY 1988

Liverpool's Anfield Rap is released ahead of the FA Cup Final. Reaching number three in the UK charts, the song was written by squad member Craig Johnston and rapper Derek B and was influenced by artists such as Eric B and Rakim, The Beatles and the Jackson 5. John Aldridge and Steve McMahon took centre stage and ITV's legendary football commentator Brian Moore even performed one verse!

SATURDAY 8th MAY 1971

Charlie George scores the winner as league champions Arsenal win the FA Cup after extra time to complete a domestic double. Steve Heighway gave Liverpool the lead less than a minute into the first period of extra time, but Eddie Kelly equalised ten minutes later before George's winner nine minutes from time. It was a disappointing season for Bill Shankly, who saw his team finish fifth in the league, too.

SATURDAY 9th MAY 1992

Graeme Souness claims his first major trophy as Liverpool manager as his side beat Sunderland 2-0 in the FA Cup Final. Michael Thomas, who had denied Liverpool a league title when he scored a last-gasp goal for Arsenal in 1989, put his side ahead two minutes after half-time, before talismanic striker Ian Rush netted Liverpool's second midway through the second half to ensure the club lift the trophy for the fifth time.

WEDNESDAY 10th MAY 1922

Having beaten Preston North End in the FA Cup Final, Huddersfield Town, who finished 14th in the league, beat Liverpool 1-0 in the Charity Shield with Tom Wilson scoring the only goal of the game for the Terriers. The game was played at Old Trafford in front of a crowd of around 20,000 and would be David Ashworth's only appearance in a final as Liverpool manager.

WEDNESDAY 10th MAY 1978

Kenny Dalglish scores the only goal of the game as Liverpool are crowned champions of Europe for the second consecutive season with a 1-0 win over Club Brugge at Wembley Stadium. Notable absences in the final for Liverpool were David Johnson, who strained his knee ligaments earlier in the season, and Tommy Smith, who had dropped a pick-axe on his foot and broken his toe. The introduction of Steve Heighway for Jimmy Case significantly changed the game, because just one minute later Dalglish received the ball from fellow Scot Graeme Souness and won the match for Liverpool just after the hour mark with a delightful chip over the Brugge keeper. The club became the first British team to win back-to-back European titles.

SATURDAY 10th MAY 1986

Two second-half goals from Ian Rush, and another from Craig Johnston, cancel out Gary Lineker's opener as Liverpool beat Everton 3-1 in the FA Cup Final. Kenny Dalglish did what Bob Paisley and Joe Fagan could not by winning the most coveted trophy in domestic football, which was only the club's third triumph in the competition in seven attempts.

TUESDAY 11th MAY 1993

Nearly 12,000 people piled into the Racecourse Ground to watch European Cup winner Joey Jones' testimonial. Four goals were evenly shared between Wrexham and Liverpool, where Jones had spent several years, along with spells at Chelsea and Huddersfield Town. The Welsh defender began his career at Wrexham before signing for Liverpool in July 1975 for £110,000. Jones then rejoined the Robins three years later, then had stints in London and Yorkshire before returning to north Wales for a third time to end his career. It is fitting that Welshman Ian Rush should get on the score-sheet for Liverpool, adding to Don Hutchison's goal.

SATURDAY 11th MAY 1996

Eric Cantona haunts Liverpool once more as he scores the only goal of the game with five minutes remaining, to hand Manchester United their ninth FA Cup triumph. The game proved to be Ian Rush's last game for Liverpool as he left the club to join Leeds United after scoring 346 goals for the club over the course of 16 years.

SATURDAY 12th MAY 1984

Southampton draw 0-0 with Birmingham City at St Andrew's and Liverpool draw 0-0 with Notts County at Meadow Lane, meaning the Division One title is won by the Anfield outfit for the third consecutive season. Liverpool effectively won the title on May 7th when they beat Coventry City 5-0 at home, as they had a much superior goal difference to Southampton and were six points clear with two games to play. All Joe Fagan's side needed was a point from their remaining two games, and they duly delivered, ensuring a 15th English championship for Liverpool.

SATURDAY 13th MAY 2006

Steven Gerrard crashes home a remarkable and sensational late equaliser to make it 3-3 as Liverpool force extra time in the FA Cup Final. Dean Ashton had doubled West Ham's lead just after Jamie Carragher had put the ball into his own net to make it 2-0 before half an hour had been played, but Djibril Cisse pulled one back for Rafael Benitez' men. Gerrard equalised for the first time nine minutes into the second half but Paul Konchesky scored with a cross-come-shot just after the hour mark to make it 3-2 before Reds' captain Gerrard let fly from 30 yards on 90 minutes to level the scores. Liverpool won 3-1 in the ensuing penalty shoot-out.

SATURDAY 14th MAY 1988

Wimbledon, who finished seventh in Division One, beat English champions Liverpool 1-0 in the FA Cup Final in front of 98,203 fans at Wembley. The only goal came from a looping Lawrie Sanchez header from Dennis Wise's free kick on 37 minutes. Wimbledon captain Dave Beasant became the first goalkeeper to save a penalty in an FA Cup Final, when he kept out John Aldridge's spot kick on the hour mark.

SATURDAY 15th MAY 1982

Following the introduction of three points for a win, Liverpool win the Division One title for the third time in four seasons after beating Tottenham Hotspur 3-1 at Anfield. Second-place Ipswich Town could have made the season go down to the final game, but they lost 3-1 at home to Nottingham Forest, meaning Liverpool went six points clear at the top of the table with one game to go, ensuring a fifth league title for Bob Paisley.

TUESDAY 16th MAY 2000

Erik Meijer scores twice in Ronnie Moran's testimonial against Celtic at Anfield – equalling the number of goals he scored during his time at the club. David Thompson and Titi Camara had also found the back of the net to help bring the score to 4-0 before defender Christian Dailly scored a consolation for the visitors. Moran, who was 66 at the time of the testimonial, made 379 appearances for Liverpool over 13 years, scoring 17 goals from full-back.

CAPTAIN FANTASTIC – STEVEN GERRARD LIFTS THE FA CUP AFTER VICTORY OVER WEST HAM UNITED (SEE 13TH MAY 2006).

WEDNESDAY 16th MAY 2001

Liverpool beat Alavés 5-4 after extra time to win the Uefa Cup and complete a treble under the charge of Gerard Houllier. Markus Babbel had given Liverpool the perfect start just four minutes into the tie at the Westfalenstadion in Dortmund, before Steven Gerrard added a second with barely 16 minutes gone. Alonso, brought on for defender Eggen, scored within four minutes of walking on the pitch, but Gary McAllister restored Liverpool's two-goal lead after Michael Owen was brought down by goalkeeper Martin Herrera. Two goals six minutes after the restart from Moreno pulled Alavés level, before Robbie Fowler put Liverpool back in front on 73 minutes. But, former Manchester United midfielder Jordi Cruyff levelled the game with just one minute left to play to force extra time – and the golden goal rule. It looked as though Alonso had scored the winner for the Spaniards, but he was ruled offside. Alavés had both Mocelin and captain Karmona sent off before Geli headed past his own keeper from a McAllister free kick.

SUNDAY 17th MAY 2009

A goal in each half, one from Steven Gerrard and another from Dirk Kuyt, give Liverpool a 2-0 win away to West Bromwich Albion. The victory puts the Reds within four points of Premier League leaders Manchester United – but sadly with just one game to play!

SATURDAY 18th MAY 1982

Champions Liverpool round off the campaign with a 0-0 draw away to Middlesbrough. The Reds had already won the league and this point meant they finished four ahead of runners-up Ipswich Town.

WEDNESDAY 19th MAY 1976

Kevin Keegan's equaliser after 15 minutes earns a draw in the away leg of the Uefa Cup Final against Club Brugge and a 4-3 aggregate victory as Liverpool win the competition for the second time in four years. Liverpool had been 2-0 down in the first leg at Anfield, but three second-half goals in the space of five minutes from Ray Kennedy, Jimmy Case and a penalty from Keegan, turned the match on its head to give the club a slight advantage for the return leg in Belgium.

SATURDAY 20th MAY 1989

Substitute Stuart McCall's 89th-minute equaliser forces extra time in the FA Cup Final at Wembley, but two goals from Ian Rush ensure victory for Liverpool over bitter local rivals Everton. John Aldridge had given Liverpool the lead after just four minutes before McCall poked the ball home, which resulted in a pitch invasion from the Everton fans. Five minutes into extra time, Rush netted his first of the game to put the Reds back in front. However, just five minutes later, McCall grabbed his second as he volleyed past Grobbelaar to score only his third Toffees goal. But, it was Rush who would have the last laugh as he headed home John Barnes' cross to score. It was the second time the Welshman had scored twice against Everton in an FA Cup Final, repeating his achievement from the 1986 final.

SATURDAY 21st MAY 1977

Three goals in five second-half minutes light up the FA Cup Final as Liverpool finish runners-up for the fourth time, after losing 2-1 to Manchester United. A Jimmy Case goal in between strikes from Stuart Pearson and Jimmy Greenhoff was all Liverpool had to celebrate at Wembley after reaching their sixth FA Cup Final, and first under Bob Paisley.

SUNDAY 21st MAY 2000

Over 35,000 supporters travelled to Lansdowne Road to watch Steve Staunton and Tony Cascarino's testimonial against an Irish XI. Staunton captained the Ireland side, which included Robbie Keane and Niall Quinn. Emile Heskey and Michael Owen got the goals for Liverpool in either half, while Cascarino scored twice late in the game for Ireland to mark his testimonial game. Keane was also on the score-sheet for the Irish who won 4-2.

SUNDAY 22nd MAY 2011

Aston Villa beat Liverpool 1-0 at Villa Park on the final day of the 2010/11 season to end the Reds' slim hopes of Europa League football. Stewart Downing's 33rd-minute goal settles a game that means Kenny Dalglish's men finish sixth in the Premier League. Tottenham claim the poisoned chalice that many consider to be fifth place and the possibility of a long Europa League campaign to boot.

WEDNESDAY 23rd MAY 1973

Despite losing 2-0, Liverpool win the Uefa Cup 3-2 on aggregate against Borussia Monchengladbach after two first-half goals from Josef Heynckles ensured a nervy finish for Bill Shankly's team. The Reds manage to hold out for the win after two goals from Kevin Keegan, and one from Larry Lloyd in the first leg at Anfield two weeks earlier, had put their side in a commanding position over the German outfit. It's the first European trophy of many for Liverpool.

WEDNESDAY 23rd MAY 2007

Two goals from Filippo Inzaghi are enough to ensure Champions League Final victory for AC Milan over Liverpool at the second attempt following their heartache in 2005. The Italian marksman netted late in either half to put the game out of reach, despite a late goal from Dirk Kuyt with one minute to go. Approximately 74,000 fans watched the final in Athens as Milan won 2-1, avoiding a repeat result from two years previously to win their seventh European title and no doubt exorcising a few demons in the process.

MONDAY 24th MAY 2004

Gerard Houllier leaves the club by mutual consent following a disappointing campaign in which Liverpool finish fourth – 30 points behind Premier League champions Arsenal. Despite winning two League Cups, one FA Cup, one Uefa Cup, and one European Super Cup, his style of football was branded one-dimensional and his youth policy was highly criticised as the Frenchman opted to spend big money on foreign signings as opposed to nurturing home-grown talent. Liverpool's first foreign manager won just over half of his games in charge.

WEDNESDAY 25th MAY 1977

Liverpool put their FA Cup heartache behind them and beat Borussia Monchengladbach 3-1 in Rome to lift the European Cup for the first time. Terry McDermott gave Liverpool the lead midway through the first half, before Allan Simonsen equalised six minutes after the break. But Tommy Smith restored the Reds' lead just after the hour mark before right-back Phil Neal put the game beyond doubt as he converted a penalty with eight minutes to go.

TOMMY SMITH — THE IRON MAN OF ANFIELD (SEE 25TH MAY 1977).

WEDNESDAY 25th MAY 2005

Liverpool win one of the most dramatic Champions League finals in the history of the competition as they take Italian giants AC Milan to a penalty shoot-out at the Atatürk Olympic Stadium in Istanbul. The tie looked bleak for Rafael Benitez's team as Paolo Maldini's first-minute opener was added to twice by Hernán Crespo in five first-half minutes to put Carlo Ancelotti's side 3-0 up before the interval. But, goals from Steven Gerrard, Vladimír Šmicer and Xabi Alonso in six minutes before the hour mark levelled the tie for Liverpool, who pulled off the most unlikely comeback in European history. In extra time Andriy Shevchenko came close to giving Milan the win, but Jerzy Dudek pulled off a fantastic double save to force penalties. Dudek re-enacted Bruce Grobbelaar's infamous 'spaghetti legs' from the 1984 European Cup Final win over Roma, in order to put off the Milan players. It was effective as Serginho and Andrea Pirlo missed from the spot before Dudek saved the crucial penalty from Shevchenko to win the Champions League for Liverpool.

SATURDAY 26th MAY 1928

George Pither leaves Liverpool after making just 12 starts for the Reds. The former Merthyr Town left-winger managed just one goal during his time at Anfield before he left to join Crewe Alexandra.

FRIDAY 26th MAY 1989

The most dramatic finale to a season imaginable sees the entire 1988/89 title race come down to one game – Liverpool versus Arsenal at Anfield. The Reds knew that a draw or defeat by a single goal would be enough to finish ahead of the second-placed Gunners in a match unusually held on a Friday evening due to re-arrangements. With the score 0-0, seven minutes after the break Alan Smith scored for Arsenal and suddenly, the Reds nerves started to show. But, right up until the last few seconds, it seemed they'd done enough – that is until Michael Thomas burst through to pick up a loose ball and fire past Bruce Grobbelaar for an incredible championship-winning goal – with just about the last kick of the game. The title went to Highbury and Anfield was left shell-shocked.

WEDNESDAY 27th MAY 1981

Left-back Alan Kennedy scores the winner with just eight minutes to go as Liverpool beat Real Madrid in the European Cup Final. Bob Paisley wins the famous trophy for the third time in five years as he writes himself into the Liverpool history books once more. The win meant that the European Cup had been won by an English club for the fifth successive season, with Nottingham Forest winning the competition in 1979 and 1980.

THURSDAY 27th MAY 1999

Right-back Rob Jones leaves Liverpool after 243 appearances for the Reds. The unlucky defender suffered numerous injuries and would otherwise have had a long career with the Reds – as it was, he was forced to retire at the age of 27. Jones did attempt to resurrect his career with West Ham United but the injuries he'd sustained throughout his career meant the move was futile.

WEDNESDAY 28th MAY 1924

William Cockburn signs for Liverpool. The central defender plays 67 times for the Reds before moving to pastures new in 1928.

WEDNESDAY 29th MAY 1985

The 1985 European Cup Final is overshadowed by the tragic death of 39 spectators following riots at the Heysel Stadium in the Belgian capital, Brussels. After both sets of supporters began to hurl missiles an hour before kick-off, violence erupted on a devastating scale that shook the world of football to its core. As some Liverpool fans charged at Juventus supporters – crossing a small wire fence separating the supporters – the Italian crowd was forced backwards towards a perimeter wall. Some people managed to flee over the top, but the wall could not take the pressure and collapsed with shocking consequences. Despite the disaster, football's grandest domestic spectacle went ahead in order to avoid further disturbances, and Juventus won 1-0 courtesy of a Michel Platini penalty on a night that more than 600 people were injured. The incident resulted in English football clubs being banned indefinitely from European competitions, but the ban was lifted at the start of the 1990/91 campaign. In the aftermath, several Liverpool fans were prosecuted for manslaughter on a shameful episode for English football.

WEDNESDAY 29th MAY 1985

Former Boot Room member and Liverpool manager Joe Fagan announces his intention to retire at the end of the season. His last game would see one of the darkest days in the club's and European football's history as Juventus' victory was overshadowed by the Heysel Stadium disaster. Fagan had led the club to its fourth European Cup the previous season with a penalty shoot-out victory over AS Roma, while also retaining the league championship and League Cup, which the Reds won for the fourth consecutive season courtesy of Graeme Souness' goal in a replay at Maine Road.

WEDNESDAY 30th MAY 1984

Alan Kennedy, hero of Liverpool's last European Cup Final, is at it again as he scores the winning penalty in the penalty shoot-out to win the European Cup for Liverpool for the fourth time. The game, played against Italian side AS Roma – at the Stadio Olimpico in Rome – is remembered for Zimbabwean goalkeeper Bruce Grobbelaar putting off the Roma penalty takers with his infamous 'spaghetti legs' routine, which led to Bruno Conti and Francesco Graziani both blazing their spot kicks over the bar. Phil Neal had given Liverpool the lead in the first half and Roberto Pruzzo equalised three minutes before half-time. It was a triumph against the odds and a famous night in the Reds' history.

SATURDAY 31st MAY 1947

Liverpool win the first Division One title since the outbreak of World War II, finishing one point clear of Manchester United. There was immense pressure on George Kay's men to deliver a result after United had thrashed Sheffield United 6-2 at Old Trafford in their final game of the season just five days earlier – and his team wouldn't disappoint. The all-important win came at Molineux as Wolverhampton Wanderers were beaten 2-1 by Liverpool, with the Reds' goals coming from Jack Balmer on 21 minutes and Albert Stubbins on 38 minutes. Many pinpoint the 1-0 victory against United at Anfield four weeks earlier as the key to the triumph, with Liverpool taking over the lead in the title race and remaining unbeaten for the remainder of the campaign.

LIVERPOOL FC
On This Day

JUNE

THURSDAY 1st JUNE 1989

Glenn Hysen joins Liverpool from Fiorentina in a £600,000 deal. The former PSV Eindhoven defender joined the club at the age of 29 and played an important role in Liverpool's championship-winning season, in which the club claimed its 18th Division One title. The Swede, capped 68 times by his country, went on to make 93 appearances for the Reds and scored three goals – one of which was the eighth in a 9-0 thrashing of Crystal Palace at Anfield on September 12th 1989.

SUNDAY 2nd JUNE 1957

Mark Lawrenson is born in Preston, England. After signing from Brighton & Hove Albion in 1981 for a fee of £900,000, Lawrenson would go on to win a variety of honours while at Liverpool, most notably the European Cup in 1984 in which the club beat Roma on penalties following a 1-1 draw at the Stadio Olimpico, Rome. The Republic of Ireland international played the entire game, but did not step up to take a penalty. Further triumphs include five English championships, three League Cups, two Charity Shields and one FA Cup in a glittering Anfield career. Lawro went on to become one of the country's leading pundits on *Match of the Day*.

MONDAY 2nd JUNE 1997

Oyvind Leonhardsen joins Liverpool from Wimbledon. Roy Evans pays £3.5m for the Norwegian midfielder whose industry makes him a popular figure among the Reds' supporters. 'Leo' plays 49 times and scores seven goals before joining Spurs after two years at Anfield.

FRIDAY 3rd JUNE 1977

After winning three Division One titles, two Uefa Cups, one FA Cup and a European Cup, Kevin Keegan leaves Liverpool to sign for German Bundesliga outfit Hamburg for £500,000. Keegan made his name at Scunthorpe United where he was a diminutive midfielder, scoring 22 goals in 141 appearances while in Lincolnshire. He was signed by Bill Shankly after Andy Beattie, Shankly's former team-mate at Preston North End, continued to rave about the young prodigy, who went on to make 323 appearances for Liverpool, scoring 100 goals.

THURSDAY 3rd JUNE 2010

After six seasons at Anfield, Rafa Benitez leaves the club by mutual consent following a poor season which results in the club finishing seventh in the Premier League. The Spaniard had a fine start to his Liverpool tenure, with the club winning one of the most dramatic and memorable Champions League finals in the history of the competition. With his side trailing 3-0 at half-time, it looked as though the tie was effectively over as a contest, but three second-half goals in the space of six minutes brought Liverpool level. Goalkeeping heroics from Jerzy Dudek, and nerves of steel, saw Benitez and Liverpool crowned European champions for the fifth time.

SUNDAY 4th JUNE 1905

David Davidson is born in Aberdeen, Scotland. The tough-tackling defender signed for Liverpool at the age of 23, as he took his first steps into English football following his transfer from Forfar Athletic. Davidson made 62 appearances for the club under the charge of George Patterson, and scored two goals against Portsmouth and West Ham United, respectively. He left Anfield in 1930 to join Newcastle United.

MONDAY 5th JUNE 1950

Son of former Liverpool manager Joe Fagan, Chris is born in Manchester, England. The defender only played twice for the club, once in a League Cup second-round tie against Mansfield Town on September 22nd 1970, coming on as a substitute for Steve Heighway. The second game was in a 2-2 draw with Manchester City in a Division One clash at Maine Road, where manager Bill Shankly fielded a relatively weak side in order to rest his first-team players ahead of a European Fairs Cup semi-final tie with Leeds United.

MONDAY 6th JUNE 1955

Goalkeeper Charlie Ashcroft leaves Liverpool to join Torquay United, having made 89 appearances for the club over nine years. He only played twice in his first season and conceded nine goals in a 7-4 victory over Chelsea, and a 5-0 defeat against Manchester United. Ashcroft became Liverpool's first-choice goalkeeper in 1951, after Cyril Sidlow left to join Notts County, and made 35 appearances, keeping seven clean sheets as the club finished 11th in Division One.

MONDAY 7th JUNE 1993

Liverpool complete the signing of Nigel Clough from Nottingham Forest in a deal worth just over £2m. The son of legendary manager Brian Clough goes on to make 44 appearances in a Liverpool shirt, scoring eight goals, two of which came in a 3-3 draw with Manchester United at Anfield, repeating his shining debut performance where he netted twice against Sheffield Wednesday. He was unable to maintain the high level of his displays and was eventually sold to struggling Manchester City.

FRIDAY 8th JUNE 1984

Javier Mascherano is born in San Lorenzo, Argentina. The fierce-tackling midfielder joined Liverpool from West Ham United for £18.6m on February 29th 2008 after impressing whilst on loan at Anfield. He made 139 appearances for the club before leaving the club on August 30th 2010 for Spanish giants Barcelona in a £22m deal.

TUESDAY 9th JUNE 1987

Watford and England winger John Barnes joins Liverpool in a £900,000 deal, having made over 200 appearances for the Hornets, scoring double figures in every campaign for the club. Barnes teamed up with England team-mate Peter Beardsley and formed a formidable partnership first with John Aldridge, and then Ian Rush, as the club went on to win a host of major honours under Kenny Dalglish. Barnes made over 400 appearances for Liverpool, scoring 108 goals in an Anfield career that spanned nine years.

FRIDAY 10th JUNE 2011

Jordan Henderson announces that he is delighted to join Liverpool after penning a deal the day before. The Sunderland midfielder is believed to cost in excess of £16m.

THURSDAY 11th JUNE 1953

Peter McDonnell is born in Kendal. The keeper signed for Liverpool from Bury in 1974 at the age of 21 and won a European Cup winners' medal, despite never playing a game for the club. McDonnell was on the bench for the 1977 final against Borussia Monchengladbach at the Stadio Olimpico, a game which Liverpool won 3-1. He moved to Oldham Athletic in 1978 where he went on to make over 100 appearances in four seasons.

JOHN BARNES – A SUPERB WINGER AND LYNCHPIN OF THE SUCCESSFUL SIDE OF THE LATE 1980s. (SEE 9TH JUNE 1987).

TUESDAY 12th JUNE 1984

Sampdoria complete the signing of Liverpool midfielder Graeme Souness for £650,000, where he teamed up with a group of aspiring young players, including Roberto Mancini. Souness had a glorious Liverpool career, winning five Division One titles and three European Cups in just six years after he arrived on Merseyside from Middlesbrough in a £352,000 transfer. He scored 55 goals in 359 appearances and won 54 caps for Scotland.

MONDAY 13th JUNE 1955

Alan Hansen is born in Sauchie, Scotland. The defender cost Liverpool £110,000 when he transferred from Partick Thistle in 1977 and immediately became an integral part of Bob Paisley's plans. In 13 years at Anfield, the Scotsman won numerous honours, including eight Division One titles and three European Cups as the club dominated not only the English game, but the continental game too. After 620 appearances in a red shirt, Hansen called time on his Liverpool career in 1990 as the club claimed its 18th English championship with a 2-1 win over Queens Park Rangers.

FRIDAY 14th JUNE 1878

Arthur Goddard is born in Heaton Norris, Stockport, England. He cost Liverpool £460 when he transferred from Glossop North End in February 1902 as a 23-year-old. Goddard made 414 appearances on the right wing for Liverpool over 13 years and scored 77 goals. He was part of the club's first-ever Division One championship-winning side in 1902, and won a second title in 1906, scoring six goals in 38 appearances under the charge of Tom Watson.

MONDAY 14th JUNE 1971

Steve Peplow leaves Liverpool having given up on winning a first-team berth at Anfield. The Liverpool-born striker was prolific at reserve level during the 1968/69 season, finding the net 19 times, and finally made his senior debut against West Ham United in November 1969, but despite two more starts, he drifts out of the picture and after a spell on loan with Swindon Town, eventually joins Tranmere Rovers where he plays 248 times and scores 48 goals over an eight-year period.

TUESDAY 15th JUNE 1999

Liverpool complete the signing of 24-year-old Dutch goalkeeper Sander Westerveld from Vitesse Arnhem in a £4m deal, becoming the most expensive goalkeeper in British transfer history. He succeeded David James and played a crucial role as Liverpool won the treble in 2001, saving Andy Johnson's penalty in the shoot-out against Birmingham City in the League Cup Final. In his first season, Westerveld conceded the fewest goals of any Premier League goalkeeper, reinforcing manager Gerard Houllier's decision to spend big money on the man who would win six caps for his country. But, after a series of mistakes, Polish goalkeeper Jerzy Dukek was brought in – along with Chris Kirkland – and Westerveld found himself surplus to requirements at Anfield, and was sold to Real Sociedad in Spain.

WEDNESDAY 16th JUNE 2004

Rafael Benitez is appointed as Liverpool manager following the departure of Gerard Houllier by mutual consent. The Spaniard had a proven track record having won the La Liga title twice with Valencia and tasting Uefa Cup success in a three-year career at the Mestalla. During his first season at Anfield, Benitez went down in history as he guided the club to Champions League victory over AC Milan, as Liverpool claimed their fifth European crown. His team had trailed 3-0 at half-time in Turkey before an astonishing second-half performance saw Liverpool pull level before a penalty shoot-out victory in Istanbul. 'Rafa' left the club by mutual consent in 2010 after only managing a seventh-place finish.

SUNDAY 17th JUNE 1990

Jordan Henderson is born in Sunderland, England. After impressing in two full seasons with home-town club Sunderland, Henderson completed his transfer to Liverpool on June 9th 2011 for an undisclosed fee, believed to be in the region of £16m. He was named as Sunderland's Young Player of the Year for two seasons running before moving to Anfield as part of Kenny Dalglish's rebuilding programme under the ownership of Fenway Sports Group. Henderson grabs his first goal for the Reds in August 2011 when he hammers home a shot against Bolton Wanderers at Anfield.

FRIDAY 18th JUNE 1971

Die-hard Liverpool fan Jason McAteer is born in Birkenhead, England. He completed his dream move to Anfield when he transferred from Bolton Wanderers for £4.5m on September 7th 1995 and went on to make 139 appearances for Liverpool in four seasons.

SUNDAY 19th JUNE 2011

Press reports suggest Liverpool and Arsenal are locked in a battle to sign Birmingham City's £12m-rated Scott Dann.

WEDNESDAY 20th JUNE 2001

John Arne Riise completes his £4m transfer from Monaco to team up with Gerard Houllier at Anfield. The Norwegian left-back was relatively unknown before he moved from France, but soon developed a reputation as being one of the most consistent defenders in the Premier League – and the owner of a ferocious left foot. He scored a debut goal for Liverpool in the European Super Cup triumph over Bayern Munich in 2001 before netting a blistering free kick against Manchester United in a 3-1 victory at Anfield, which almost uprooted the goal posts. Riise was part of the Champions League-winning side in 2005, before moving to Roma in 2008 after making 348 appearances for Liverpool.

SUNDAY 21st JUNE 1964

Son of former Liverpool wing-half Roy Saunders, Dean is born in Swansea, Wales. He made his name at Oxford United under the charge of former Liverpool defender Mark Lawrenson where he scored 33 goals in 73 appearances before he was sold, against Lawrenson's wishes, to Derby County. Soon after, he transferred to Liverpool for £2.9m on July 19th 1991, but he could only manage 25 goals in 61 games and was sold to Aston Villa for £2.5m in September 1992.

WEDNESDAY 22nd JUNE 1898

Albert Whitehurst is born in Fenton, Stoke-on-Trent, England. The striker came to Liverpool in May 1928 with a fantastic reputation having netted 116 goals in 168 games for Division Three (North) side Rochdale. However, with opportunities limited, he joined Bradford City less than a year after signing for the club.

THURSDAY 23rd JUNE 1955

Powerful right-back John Molyneux joins Liverpool from Chester City for £4,500 with a reputation as a no-nonsense defender. In a seven-year career at Anfield, Molyneux made 249 appearances, scoring just the three goals against; Brighton & Hove Albion, Aston Villa and Southend United. All of his goals came in the first half from open play. He left to re-join Chester in 1962.

SATURDAY 24th JUNE 1967

Goalkeeper Ray Clemence joins Liverpool from Scunthorpe United for £18,000 as Bill Shankly looks to bolster his defensive line. After becoming first-choice goalkeeper ahead of Tommy Lawrence, Clemence only missed six games in 11 years and won a host of awards including three European Cups and five Division One titles. He spent 14 years at Anfield after joining as an 18-year-old and made 665 appearances for the club, becoming one of the most celebrated players in Liverpool's history.

MONDAY 25th JUNE 1973

Jamie Redknapp, son of former West Ham United midfielder and manager, Harry, is born in Barton-on-Sea, England. Redknapp junior made a name for himself at AFC Bournemouth, who were being managed by his father at the time, before Kenny Dalglish snapped up the young prodigy at the age of 17 in a £350,000 deal, making Redknapp one of the most expensive teenagers in Britain at the time. While at Anfield he made 308 appearances, scoring 41 goals, and won 17 caps for England before moving to Tottenham Hotspur on a free transfer. Injuries took their toll on Redknapp's career and he was forced to retire early, becoming a pundit on Sky Sports in order to remain in the game.

FRIDAY 26th JUNE 2009

Energetic right-back Glen Johnson completes his £17.5m transfer from Portsmouth as Liverpool manager Rafael Benitez looks to strengthen his defence with the addition of pace and attacking flair. The England international started his career at West Ham United before joining the Chelsea revolution under Roman Abramovic. He made 70 appearances in three seasons before Portsmouth signed him on loan. The south coast side made the deal permanent after Johnson impressed and he made 71 appearances after completing his transfer.

MONDAY 27th JUNE 2011

Rumours abound in the press that Liverpool are set to sign Blackpool's Charlie Adam and Aston Villa winger Stewart Downing. The pair are rumoured to cost in the region of £30m combined as Kenny Dalglish continues his rebuilding programme. Though the reports are proved accurate, neither player will actually join the Reds for another couple of weeks.

MONDAY 28th JUNE 1897

Joe Keetley is born in Derby, England. Having only signed for Accrington Stanley five months previously, Keetley completed his £1,200 transfer to Division One champions Liverpool in November 1923 where he would only make nine appearances in the midfield. He scored his first goal for the club on Boxing Day 1923 in a 2-1 defeat at St James' Park against Newcastle United before getting the New Year off to a flyer as he scored in Liverpool's 3-1 victory over Chelsea at Anfield.

THURSDAY 29th JUNE 2006

French midfielder Bruno Cheyrou leaves Liverpool to join Rennes after being loaned out to Marseille, and then Bordeaux. Neither side were impressed by the midfielder, originally dubbed the new Zinedine Zidane, who made 48 appearances for Liverpool before being deemed surplus to requirements when new manager Rafael Benitez arrived from Valencia. Cheyrou scored five goals in his time at Anfield, two of which came in an FA Cup tie against Newcastle United.

SATURDAY 30th JUNE 1917

Harry Eastham is born in Blackpool, England. He started his career as an amateur at Blackpool, where his father made a name for himself, before he was snapped up by George Patterson in February 1936. Eastham went on to play 68 times for Liverpool and scored four goals before he moved to Tranmere Rovers in 1948. His Liverpool career was interrupted by the outbreak of World War II.

TUESDAY 30th JUNE 2009

Winger Paul Anderson joins Nottingham Forest after failing to break into the first team at Anfield. The Leicester-born youngster is part of Liverpool's successful FA Youth Cup side of 2006 and is later loaned to Swansea City and Forest before joining the latter for £250,000 in 2009.

LIVERPOOL FC
On This Day

JULY

FRIDAY 1st JULY 1983

Bob Paisley retires as the most successful manager in Liverpool's history after guiding the club to a sixth league championship under his charge. He won 307 of 535 games, three of which were European Cup finals against Borussia Monchengladbach, Club Brugge and Real Madrid, the only man in the history of the competition to coach three winning sides. The only trophy Paisley failed to win was the FA Cup, in which he came runner-up to Manchester United in 1977. He was the first Liverpool manager to win the League Cup, and he repeated the feat another two times.

THURSDAY 1st JULY 2010

Liverpool appoint Roy Hodgson as manager following the departure of Rafael Benitez by mutual consent. Hodgson had a proven track record in English football, having led Fulham to the Europa League Final the previous campaign and had also managed Malmö, Copenhagen and Inter Milan. Hodgson tried his luck as an international manager, first with the United Arab Emirates, and then Finland, before being enticed into his first Premier League job by Mohamed Al-Fayed at Fulham. Unfortunately, his time at Liverpool was short-lived and he left the club by mutual consent on January 8th 2011.

FRIDAY 2nd JULY 2010

Israeli midfielder Yossi Benayoun joins Chelsea in a deal worth £5.5m after spending three years at Anfield. He signed for Liverpool from West Ham United in July 2007 for £5m after making 72 appearances for the Hammers in two seasons, scoring eight goals. The former Racing Santander playmaker made his name while at Maccabi Haifa, where he scored more than 70 goals in four seasons. In 134 games for Liverpool, he got his name on the score-sheet 29 times, and is the only player to score a hat-trick in the Premier League, Champions League and FA Cup.

MONDAY 3rd JULY 2006

Academy product David Raven leaves the Reds to join Carlisle United after failing to progress from the reserves. The centre-back played 11 times for Tranmere Rovers on loan before leaving for Blundell Park on a permanent basis after just four senior appearances with the first team.

TUESDAY 3rd JULY 2007

Fans' favourite Luis Garcia leaves Liverpool to go back to his native Spain and re-join Atletico Madrid for the second time. The tricky winger joined Liverpool from Barcelona in August 2004 in a £6m deal and emerged as one of Rafael Benitez's key players, along with fellow compatriot Xabi Alonso, who had joined from Real Sociedad. Garcia played the entire game as Liverpool took the dramatic 2005 Champions League Final to penalties against AC Milan. He signed for Atletico at the age of 29 after spending three years at Anfield.

MONDAY 4th JULY 1983

'Supersub' David Fairclough leaves Liverpool after eight years with the club. The ginger-haired striker earned his nickname because of his penchant for finding the net when coming on as a substitute – he managed the feat 18 times in 62 appearances off the bench. Fairclough scored a total of 54 goals in 155 games for the Reds but never really managed to nail down a starting place and was forced to move on.

WEDNESDAY 4th JULY 2007

Having just offloaded Luis Garcia to Atletico Madrid, striker Fernando Torres comes in the opposite direction as Rafael Benitez signs the Spain international for £20.2m. Torres soon became a Kop favourite as he began to score goals galore, finishing his first season with 33 in 46 games. Injuries limited his appearances during his second campaign, but he still managed 17 goals in 38 games. A further 31 goals in 56 games followed over the course of the next two seasons before Torres completed his British transfer record £50m move to Chelsea to become the fourth most expensive player in world football.

WEDNESDAY 5th JULY 2006

After 61 appearances in a Liverpool shirt, Fernando Morientes departs Anfield after a less-than-successful spell with the club. The striker arrived at Liverpool with a reputation for being one of Europe's top marksmen, but was unable to produce the same form that made him so deadly in La Liga, managing just 12 goals for the club. He completed a £3m move to Valencia, less than half the fee Real Madrid commanded when he was sold to Liverpool in January 2004.

MONDAY 6th JULY 1992

David James completes his £1m transfer from Watford as manager Graeme Souness earmarks the goalkeeper as a fantastic prospect for the future, having made 89 appearances for the Hornets. He followed in the footsteps of John Barnes, who arrived at Anfield via Vicarage Road five years earlier for roughly the same fee. James went on to make 277 appearances for Liverpool before being replaced by Dutchman Sander Westerveld after a series of high profile errors. He moved to Aston Villa in 1999 for £1.8m.

THURSDAY 7th JULY 2011

Liverpool complete the signing of Charlie Adam from relegated Blackpool in an £8.5m deal. Adam had been extremely impressive for the Seasiders and played an important role as Ian Holloway led them out of the Championship and into the Premier League, via the play-offs. He scored the winning goal in the 3-2 play-off final victory over favourites Cardiff City before scoring 12 goals in his debut Premiership season. The Scotsman was chased by Tottenham Hotspur manager Harry Redknapp during the 2011 January transfer window, but Adam opted to stay at Bloomfield Road to help Blackpool maintain their top-flight status. He was unsuccessful as the Tangerines were relegated following a 4-2 defeat to Manchester United at Old Trafford.

TUESDAY 8th JULY 1980

Robbie Keane is born in Dublin, Ireland. Rafael Benitez brought the Irishman to Liverpool in a £19m deal from Tottenham Hotspur on July 28th 2008 after Keane had built a reputation as being one of the most prolific strikers in the Premier League. He began his career at Wolverhampton Wanderers before moving to Coventry City in 1999. After a year at Highfield Road, he moved to Inter Milan, managed at the time by World Cup winner Marco Tardelli. Keane spent just one season in Italy before moving back to England where he joined Leeds United. Spurs paid £7m for his services in 2002 and he became a regular goalscorer at White Hart Lane. He netted 107 goals in 254 games for the north London club before joining Liverpool where he could only manage seven goals in 28 appearances. He rejoined Tottenham in January 2009 for £12m, later playing for West Ham United and then LA Galaxy in 2011.

WEDNESDAY 9th JULY 2003

Australian midfielder Harry Kewell signs for Liverpool from Leeds United in a £5m deal having become one of the most feared wingers in the Premier League during his time at Elland Road. Injuries hindered his Anfield career and he was forced to be substituted in three consecutive finals; the 2005 League Cup, the 2005 Champions League and the 2006 FA Cup. He made 139 appearances in a red shirt before joining Turkish champions Galatasaray in 2008 after a successful career at Anfield.

THURSDAY 10th JULY 1997

Paul Ince completes his £4.2m transfer from Italian giants Inter Milan (committing the 'ultimate crime' in the eyes of Manchester United fans) to join Liverpool. Ince had made himself noticed after impressive performances for West Ham United when he graduated from their academy, and was soon snapped up by Sir Alex Ferguson at Man United. Inter bought the midfielder for £7.5m after he made over 200 appearances for United but after two seasons in Milan with Roy Hodgson, Ince returned to England at Anfield where he made 81 appearances before signing for Middlesbrough.

TUESDAY 11th JULY 2006

Dietmar Hamann joins Bolton Wanderers – but then signs for Manchester City 24 hours later in a bizarre transfer from Liverpool. The popular German midfielder had played 283 times for the Reds and scored 11 goals during his seven years at Anfield but his decision to quit Bolton after one day left the Trotters fuming.

FRIDAY 11th JULY 2008

Portsmouth re-sign Peter Crouch in a deal worth up to £11m. The south coast club agreed to pay £9m up front, with £2m in bonuses for appearances and goals. His first spell at Pompey resulted in 19 goals from 39 games during the club's 2001/02 Division One campaign. On July 20th 2005, Crouch completed a £7m transfer to Liverpool from Southampton, and he managed 42 goals in 138 appearances while at Anfield. A quarter of his goals came in the last 15 minutes of a game, and he managed one hat-trick while at the club in a 4-1 victory over Arsenal at Anfield in March 2007.

FRIDAY 12th JULY 1974

Ray Kennedy's arrival at Liverpool in a £180,000 deal is completely overshadowed by the news that manager Bill Shankly – the man who signed him – is resigning. Kennedy came to Anfield as a striker having proven himself at Arsenal. But, due to the form of John Toshack, Kennedy's opportunities as a striker were limited. Manager Bob Paisley's masterstroke to employ Kennedy as a left winger lengthened his career and he went on to make 393 appearances for Liverpool and even gained international recognition from England manager Don Revie when he earned his first of 17 caps against Wales in 1976.

FRIDAY 12th JULY 1974

After 783 games on the touchline, Bill Shankly retires as Liverpool manager in order to spend more time with his family. Despite failing to retain the Division One title, finishing five points behind Leeds United, Shankly led his side to FA Cup victory over Newcastle United. Two goals from future Toon favourite Kevin Keegan, either side of a Steve Highway strike, ensured Shankly's reign would go out on a winning note. It was his second FA Cup triumph, adding to his three league championships, one Uefa Cup and four Charity Shields having also won the Second Division title in 1962.

FRIDAY 13th JULY 1979

Craig Bellamy is born in Cardiff, Wales. Controversy seems to follow Bellamy around like a shadow, and it was the same in his spell at Liverpool. His volatile attitude often landed him in trouble, and during a club training session in Portugal in February 2007, he allegedly attacked team-mate John Arne Riise with a golf club. He left for West Ham United at the end of the season for £7.5m after scoring only nine goals in 42 games over two years after signing from Blackburn Rovers.

TUESDAY 13th JULY 1982

After 15 months as a Liverpool player, Kevin Sheedy elects to quit Anfield for Goodison Park having failed to win a regular starting place in the Reds' first XI. The cultured Republic of Ireland midfielder carves out a great career with the Toffees, playing 368 games and scoring 97 goals. He played just five times for Liverpool during his stay.

THE SHANKLY GATES — A MEMORIAL BEFITTING THE MAN WHO MADE LIVERPOOL FC THE CLUB IT IS TODAY (SEE 12TH JULY 1974).

TUESDAY 14th JULY 1987

Liverpool manager Kenny Dalglish completes the signing of Newcastle United striker Peter Beardsley in a £1.9m deal. The England international had scored 61 goals for the Magpies in four years at St James' Park before moving to Anfield at the age of 26. During his four seasons with Liverpool he made 175 appearances, scoring 59 goals as he teamed up with John Barnes, who arrived in the same summer. In 1991, Beardsley joined local rivals Everton for £1m after Dean Saunders' arrival at Anfield cost the former Vancouver Whitecaps striker his place in the first team.

FRIDAY 15th JULY 2011

Aston Villa and England winger Stewart Downing joins Liverpool in a deal rumoured to be in the region of £20m as manager Kenny Dalglish continues his summer spending spree in his second spell as manager. Downing arrived with a proven track record for creating goals after building a fine reputation during his time at Middlesbrough, and then Aston Villa. His form resulted in a call-up to the England team, albeit under former Boro boss Steve McLaren. However, he managed to retain his place under Fabio Capello and attracted attention from some of England's top clubs before completing his move to Anfield.

THURSDAY 16th JULY 1998

Gerard Houllier joins the club as joint manager alongside Roy Evans after a spell in charge of the French national side and French youth side. He won six major trophies while at the helm of Liverpool, including two League Cups, a Uefa Cup and an FA Cup. He was manager as the club won the treble in 2001, but parted ways with the club by mutual consent in 2004.

TUESDAY 17th JULY 2007

Mark Gonzalez leaves Liverpool after just one full season. The £1.5m signing had to wait more than a year to play for the Reds after signing in 2005 due to protracted work permit problems. After spending a year on loan with Real Betis prior to his move to Anfield, it was the La Liga side that came in for him a year later.

TUESDAY 17th JULY 2001

After just one season at Anfield, German left-back Christian Ziege departs for Tottenham Hotspur after the improvement in form of Jamie Carragher, and a series of injuries, blighted his Liverpool career. The European Championship 1996 winner was more than capable of playing left midfield, and marked his Liverpool career with two goals, one in a 3-2 defeat to Leeds United at Elland Road, and his next the first in an 8-0 mauling of Stoke City in a League Cup tie at the Britannia Stadium. He made 32 appearances for Liverpool following his arrival from Middlesbrough in a £5.5m deal before moving to White Hart Lane.

TUESDAY 18th JULY 2000

Nick Barmby moves across Stanley Park in a transfer worth £6m from Everton. The midfielder spent four seasons with the Toffees making over 130 appearances, scoring 24 goals. His form at previous club Middlesbrough had earned him an England call-up, and a £5.75m transfer to Goodison Park. Barmby became a key figure in Gerard Houllier's plans when he arrived at Anfield and was part of the treble-winning team of 2001. He left Liverpool for Leeds United in 2002 having scored eight goals in 58 games.

FRIDAY 19th JULY 1991

Wales international striker Dean Saunders joins Liverpool from Derby County in a £2.9m deal. He made his name at Swansea City where he graduated through the academy into the first team and narrowly helped the club avoid a third successive relegation in 1985. Brighton & Hove Albion snapped up the striker on a free transfer at the end of the season before he moved on to Oxford United two years later. He flourished under the management of former Liverpool defender Mark Lawrenson and was eventually sold, against Lawrenson's will, to Derby County. From there Liverpool came calling, but after two seasons and 25 goals, Saunders was sold to Aston Villa for £2.5m.

WEDNESDAY 19th JULY 2005

Liverpool ease past Total Network Solutions in the first leg of the Champions League qualifier at Wrexham's Racecourse Ground. Goals from Djibril Cisse, and two late strikes in two minutes from Steven Gerrard, give the Reds the expected margin of victory.

WEDNESDAY 20th JULY 2005

Peter Crouch completes his £7m transfer from Southampton to join the 'Rafalution' under the charge of Spanish manager Rafael Benitez. The former Valencia number one wanted to add some much needed steel to the Liverpool frontline and, having impressed during his one season with the Saints following his £2.5m move from Aston Villa, the tall hitman made the move to Merseyside. The goals did not flow as hoped, and after just 42 strikes in 134 appearances, Crouch departed for Portsmouth in 2008.

WEDNESDAY 21st JULY 2010

Joe Cole joins Liverpool from Chelsea on a free transfer. The England midfielder was Roy Hodgson's first proper signing but Cole's debut is anything but memorable after being sent off after 45 minutes against Arsenal at Anfield. Cole's season never really ignites and he never gets anywhere near the form that made him a Chelsea and England favourite.

THURSDAY 22nd JULY 1993

Neil 'Razor' Ruddock signs for Liverpool in a deal worth £2.5m from Tottenham. The tough, uncompromising defender cut an imposing figure on the pitch and his no-nonsense approach made him a player you either loved or hated. He had ability and could ping accurate passes to turn defence into attack with great effect and it's fair to say he enjoyed every minute of his time at Anfield. Ruddock played 152 times and scored 12 goals before returning to London – initially on loan with QPR – before signing permanently for West Ham United in 1998.

WEDNESDAY 23rd JULY 2008

Albert Riera joins Liverpool from Espanyol for £8m. The Spanish winger had played in England previously for Manchester City, but the cash-strapped Blues couldn't turn his loan deal into a permanent deal and he returned to Spain instead. Riera had a good first season with the Reds, but his outspoken comments of Rafa Benitez's management style led to him being transfer-listed and eventually sold to Olympiacos after less than two years with the Reds. He made 56 appearances and scored five goals during a decent spell on Merseyside.

WEDNESDAY 24th JULY 2007

Australian youngster Nicky Rizzo is sold to Crystal Palace for a nominal fee. Rizzo was snapped up by the Reds from Sydney Olympic but failed to progress as hoped and left Anfield for several years with lower league clubs before he returned to Australia in 2007.

THURSDAY 25th JULY 2008

David N'Gog joins Liverpool from Paris St Germain for a fee of £1.5m. The French forward is signed as cover for Fernando Torres and the Spaniard's injury problems see N'Gog appear regularly during his first three years at Anfield. By the end of the 2010/11 campaign, N'Gog had clocked up an impressive 94 starts, scoring 19 goals during that period.

TUESDAY 26th JULY 2005

Jamie Carragher scores his first goal for more than six years as Liverpool beat FBK Kaunus 3-1 in the Champions League qualifying round, first leg. Djibril Cisse opens the Reds' account on 26 minutes before Carragher breaks his marathon duck three minutes later. Steven Gerrard scores a third from the penalty spot on 53 minutes in a game that sees Mohamed Sissoko and Peter Crouch both make their Reds' debut.

WEDNESDAY 27th JULY 1938

Scottish teenager Billy Liddell joins Liverpool aged 16 – by the time he leaves the club, he is an Anfield legend. Because of the war, it would be seven years before the promising young forward made his debut, by which time he'd filled out and was as strong as an ox. Having honed his skills playing wartime games, he hit the ground running for the Reds and never looked back. Initially deployed on the left wing, when Liddell was given the captaincy and played as a striker, the goals flowed and he became indispensable to the club. After breaking the club's appearance record, Liddell began finding a place in the starting XI harder to come by and at the age of 39 – just before Bill Shankly's revolution was about to begin – Liddell retired. He made 534 appearances and scored 233 goals during his 21 years at Anfield.

TUESDAY 28th JULY 1992

Irish midfielder Ray Houghton leaves Liverpool after five years on Merseyside. The Glasgow-born former Fulham star made 202 appearances during his time with the Reds, with numerous spectacular goals among the 38 he scored in a red shirt. Houghton left to join Aston Villa with many feeling Graeme Souness let him leave too early.

THURSDAY 29th JULY 2010

Two David N'Gog goals give Liverpool a 2-0 lead in the third Europa League qualifying round against FK Rabotnicki in Skopje. It's new boss Roy Hodgson's first game in charge and he couldn't have asked for a more comfortable introduction into life at Anfield with N'Gog scoring in each half.

FRIDAY 30th JULY 1999

Paul Ince leaves Liverpool after just over two years at Anfield. The former West Ham United and Manchester United midfielder cost Roy Evans £4.2m from Inter Milan and was installed as skipper for the Reds, but his tenure failed to yield any silverware and after 81 appearances and 17 goals, he was allowed to join Middlesbrough after an uncomfortable relationship with new boss Gerard Houllier deteriorated.

FRIDAY 31st JULY 1992

Barry Venison calls time on his Liverpool career exactly six years after signing from Sunderland for £200,000. Venison, despite his mullet hairstyle, has a successful stay on Merseyside playing at both right and left-back and clocking up 158 appearances and scoring three goals. It was surprising that a former Sunderland skipper would choose Newcastle as his next destination after Liverpool but it proved a wise choice as Kevin Keegan moved Venison into midfield with such effect that he won two England caps.

MONDAY 31st JULY 2006

Fabio Aurelio joins Liverpool from Valencia on a free transfer. It's a smart piece of business by Rafa Benitez with the Brazilian left winger/full-back coveted by many clubs around Europe. Injuries cause Aurelio to drift in and out of the Liverpool side but Roy Hodgson awarded him a new two-year deal in 2010 and he had made 131 appearances by August 2011.

LIVERPOOL FC
On This Day

AUGUST

SATURDAY 1st AUGUST 1998

The man who once dramatically stole the league title away from Liverpool at Anfield with a last-minute winner for Arsenal, moves on after eight years with the Reds. Midfielder Michael Thomas joined the Reds in 1991 from the Gunners at a cost of £1.5m and for his first few seasons he was on the periphery of the first team as injuries hampered his progress. When he finally established himself, Thomas proved adaptable from midfield to full-back and managed to clock up 163 appearances over a seven-year period, scoring 12 goals. The highlight of his stay was undoubtedly his spectacular FA Cup Final goal against Sunderland during his first year on Merseyside.

TUESDAY 2nd AUGUST 2005

Steven Gerrard's rich scoring vein continues with his seventh goal of the season – all scored in the Champions League qualifiers. The latest strike comes in a 2-0 win over Lithuanian side FBK Kaunus in the third-round second leg tie at Anfield. Gerrard's goal comes on 77 minutes and Djibril Cisse – also having a great start to the campaign – scores the second nine minutes later to complete a 5-1 aggregate victory.

WEDNESDAY 3rd AUGUST 2011

Thomas Ince joins Notts County after failing to break into the first team at Anfield. The son of former Reds skipper Paul Ince signed for Liverpool in 2008, aged 16, and made his one senior appearance against Northampton Town in 2010 as a 106th-minute substitute.

SUNDAY 4th AUGUST 1957

John Wark is born in Glasgow. Though he will be mainly remembered for his exploits with Ipswich Town, Wark joined Liverpool from the Suffolk side in 1984 at a cost of £450,000. A replacement for the Italy-bound Graeme Souness, Wark had an incredible first season, ending as top scorer with 27 goals – not bad for a midfielder! Injuries hampered the remaining years of his time at Anfield and when Jan Molby's emergence limited his first-team chances, Wark returned to Ipswich in 1988 having scored 42 goals in just 108 games. Bob Paisley once claimed Wark's timing in the box was so good, you could set you watch by him. High praise indeed.

WEDNESDAY 5th AUGUST 2009

Fans' favourite Xabi Alonso joins Real Madrid after five memorable years at Anfield. Signed for £10.7m from Real Sociedad, Alonso soon became a huge hit at Anfield with his graceful style, dignity and penchant for truly spectacular goals – twice finding the net from his own half, once against Luton at Kenilworth Road and another against Newcastle United at Anfield. He scored in the Champions League Final against AC Milan in 2005 but always dreamed of a return to La Liga before the end of his career and in 2009, he got his wish, signing for Real Madrid in a deal rumoured to be worth £30m. Alonso scored 19 goals and played 210 times for the Reds and will always be fondly remembered at Anfield.

THURSDAY 6th AUGUST 1936

George Patterson retires as Liverpool manager following eight years in charge of the club and returns to his position as secretary. He joined the club as Watson's assistant in 1908 before taking on an off-the-field role. After being appointed as Liverpool manager on Wednesday 7th March 1928, his first game was at Highbury where Liverpool lost 6-3 to a strong Arsenal side. Patterson's first victory came a month later as Liverpool beat Huddersfield Town 4-2 at Leeds Road.

SATURDAY 7th AUGUST 1971

Leicester City beat Liverpool 1-0 in the Charity Shield, with the goal coming from defender Steve Whitworth. The Foxes were invited to play in the Shield – after winning the Division Two title in the previous campaign – because Arsenal, who had won the domestic double, had European commitments. A crowd of 25,104 spectators watch at Filbert Street and leave delighted with what was a shock victory.

MONDAY 7th AUGUST 1995

Steve McManaman scores a hat-trick for Liverpool against a Yeovil Town XI as they go on to win 7-1 in Nicky Tanner's testimonial. Tanner made 59 appearances for the Reds after moving from Bristol Rovers for £200,000 in August 1988. But, sadly, a back injury cut his Anfield career short and he was forced to retire. Robbie Fowler, Stig Inge Bjornebye, Jamie Redknapp and Nigel Clough got the other goals in the rout at Huish Park.

SATURDAY 8th AUGUST 1992

Liverpool lose one of the most entertaining FA Charity Shield matches as Leeds United win the annual curtain-raiser 4-3 at Wembley. The Reds goals come from Ian Rush, Dean Saunders, and a Gordon Strachan own goal, while Tony Dorigo and an Eric Cantona hat-trick edges the game for Leeds.

SATURDAY 9th AUGUST 1980

Terry McDermott scores the only goal as Liverpool win the Charity Shield for the fifth time. Around 90,000 spectators turn out at Wembley Stadium to watch the English champions face FA Cup winners and Division Two outfit West Ham United, who had beat Arsenal 1-0 in the final, courtesy of a Trevor Brooking goal in the previous campaign's competition.

SUNDAY 9th AUGUST 1992

Eric Cantona steals the headlines as he blows Liverpool away with a hat-trick in the Charity Shield. The Frenchman, who joined Leeds United from Nimes, netted twice in the last 15 minutes to put the Division One champions 4-2 ahead, before a Gordon Strachan own goal with one minute to go made for a nervy finish as Liverpool pushed for an equaliser that never came, and the game finished 4-3.

MONDAY 9th AUGUST 1993

Anfield is treated to just the one goal from Neil Ruddock, as Liverpool beat Newcastle United 1-0 in Ronnie Whelan's testimonial. Jamie Redknapp, Nigel Clough and Ian Rush were all on show for Whelan's charity match, which was played in front of over 21,000 fans. Whelan played nearly 500 games for Liverpool over a career that spanned 13 years, in which he won numerous trophies, including six league championships.

FRIDAY 9th AUGUST 1996

Jan Molby's testimonial is overshadowed by an altercation between Robbie Fowler and Björn van der Doelen, in which the referee advises Liverpool manager Roy Evans to substitute Fowler. PSV Eindhoven won the game 3-2 at Anfield in front of little over 8,000 spectators. Stan Collymore and Stig Inge Bjornebye got the goals for the hosts to mark Molby's testimonial, in which he gave all the money raised to charity.

WEDNESDAY 9th AUGUST 2006

Craig Bellamy scores on his Liverpool debut following his £6m move from Blackburn Rovers. Bellamy has a season full of controversy and manages nine goals in 42 appearances before being sold to Manchester City for £14m just a year later.

SATURDAY 10th AUGUST 1974

Ian Callaghan scores the winner as Liverpool beat Leeds United 6-5 in a penalty shoot-out at Wembley Stadium. Phil Boersma had given Bob Paisley's team the lead after just 19 minutes, but a Trevor Cherry equaliser 20 minutes from time forced penalties. As both teams scored five successful spot kicks to force sudden death, Leeds goalkeeper David Harvey stepped up and hit the bar before Callaghan kept his nerve to win the Charity Shield for Liverpool.

FRIDAY 10th AUGUST 1984

Bob Paisley identifies Kenny Dalglish as the man to replace Kevin Keegan at Anfield and pays £440,000 to bring the gifted Scot to Merseyside from Celtic. Dalglish proves an instant hit with the Kop and so begins a love affair that was still going strong in 2011. Only once in his first six seasons did he fail to net at least 20 goals for the Reds. He scored the winning goal in the 1978 European Cup Final against Bruges at Wembley and was an ever-present five times in his first nine seasons with Liverpool. He later became player-manager and after leaving Anfield, returned as boss in 2010. One of – if not, the – greatest Liverpool player, Dalglish has won pretty much everything there is to win as a player, and later as manager, and his enthusiasm and smile remains as infectious today as it was more than 40 years ago when he first signed.

SATURDAY 11th AUGUST 1979

Pat Jennings puts on a resilient display in the Arsenal goal, but it is not enough to stop a rampant Liverpool side who run out 3-1 winners in the Charity Shield. Terry McDermott was in inspired form for Liverpool as he scored either side of a Kenny Dalglish goal, before Alan Sunderland scored a mere consolation for the Gunners, who had beaten Manchester United in the FA Cup the previous season.

TUESDAY 11th AUGUST 1992

Ian Rush scores twice as Liverpool beat Leeds United 4-1 in a testimonial for Jim Beglin, who played for both clubs in his career, which was unfortunately cut short due to injury. The Irishman, who won 15 caps for his country, suffered a horrific broken leg during the 1987 Merseyside derby when Gary Stevens lunged in high and late. Beglin never really recovered and just a year later injured his knee cartilage in a reserve game, effectively ending his career. Leeds snapped up the defender, but he only made a handful of appearances for the Whites before calling it a day in 1991 after just 11 years in the game. Jamie Redknapp and Dean Saunders scored either side of Rush's double.

SUNDAY 11th AUGUST 2002

Gilberto Silva scores the only goal of the game as Arsenal win the Charity Shield for the 14th time. It was Liverpool's 20th appearance in the competition and the club had won the Shield on no less than 14 occasions themselves, but they were unable to overcome a strong Gunners side who were managed by Arsène Wenger. Arsenal would go on to finish second in this campaign, while Liverpool could only manage a fifth-place finish in a disappointing season for Gerard Houllier.

TUESDAY 12th AUGUST 1969

For the fourth successive year Liverpool take on Manchester City in one of the first two games of the season and 51,959 Anfield fans are treated to a cracker as the Reds go in front after just two minutes through Ian St John. City claw their way back into the game and threaten to take both points until Roger Hunt scores on 83 minutes and St John's second goal two minutes from time ensures Bill Shankly's side win 3-2.

SATURDAY 12th AUGUST 1989

Peter Beardsley scores the only goal as Liverpool win the Charity Shield for a second consecutive season, and the 12th time overall. The win is scant consolation for Kenny Dalglish's side who were narrowly beaten to the Division One title by Arsenal in the previous campaign. The Gunners won the English championship on goals scored after a last-gasp Michael Thomas goal at Anfield ensured that the teams were level on goal difference.

SUNDAY 12th AUGUST 2001

Michael Owen hits a 16th-minute winner as Liverpool win the Charity Shield for the 14th time, beating Manchester United 2-1 at the Millennium Stadium. Gary McAllister scored a second-minute penalty to give Liverpool the perfect start, before Owen doubled the lead. Dutch striker Ruud van Nistelrooy scored on his debut for the Red Devils, but it was a mere consolation as Liverpool won another trophy under Gerard Houllier.

SATURDAY 13th AUGUST 1966

A solitary goal in the ninth minute from Roger Hunt is enough to see league champions Liverpool beat FA Cup winners Everton in the Charity Shield at Goodison Park. The Toffees had beaten Sheffield Wednesday in the final 3-2 the previous season. Before the game, Hunt, Alan Ball and Ray Wilson paraded the World Cup around the stadium to 63,329 spectators after England's heroics during the summer.

SATURDAY 13th AUGUST 1977

The Charity Shield is shared once more as Liverpool play out a goalless draw with Manchester United at Wembley Stadium. It was the 55th Charity Shield and Liverpool's eighth overall, whereas United were making their tenth appearance in the competition after becoming the first team to win the trophy in 1908.

SUNDAY 13th AUGUST 2006

Liverpool beat Chelsea 2-1 in the last Community Shield to be played at the Millennium Stadium after the construction of the new Wembley Stadium. John Arne Riise gave the Reds the lead just nine minutes into the tie before Andriy Shevchenko netted a debut goal for the opposition following his £30m move from AC Milan. Crouch beat Carlo Cudicini to earn Rafael Benitez his first Community Shield, Liverpool's 15th.

SATURDAY 14th AUGUST 1965

A crowd of almost 50,000 see a late goal from Liverpool captain Ron Yeats ensure the Charity Shield is shared for a second consecutive season. The mercurial George Best and David Herd scored the goals for Matt Busby's Manchester United, while Willie Stevenson had got the other for Bill Shankly's men as the game finished 2-2 at Old Trafford.

SATURDAY 14th AUGUST 1971

Kevin Keegan scores on his Liverpool debut – after joining from Scunthorpe United – against Nottingham Forest at Anfield. Keegan takes just 12 minutes to open his account in the 3-1 opening-day victory.

SATURDAY 14th AUGUST 1976

John Toshack scores the only goal of the game as Liverpool win their fifth Charity Shield, a third Shield that has not been shared. Division Two outfit Southampton beat Manchester United in the FA Cup Final to earn their place in the Charity Shield, but were unable to pull off another shock result by beating the English champions and Uefa Cup winners at Wembley Stadium.

TUESDAY 14th AUGUST 1990

Liverpool manager Kenny Dalglish's testimonial at Anfield ends in a 3-1 win for the Reds over Spanish outfit Real Sociedad. The Scotsman made over 500 appearances for the club before becoming manager in 1985, after winning six Division One titles and three European Cups during his time as a player. The striker netted 172 goals whilst at Liverpool, and another player who was never short of goals, Ian Rush, scored twice on the night. This added to a goal from Steve McMahon, to round off a terrific evening for Dalglish. Kenny's record at Celtic was even better; the striker netted 167 times in 269 appearances for the east Glasgow club.

SATURDAY 15th AUGUST 1964

The Charity Shield is shared between Liverpool and West Ham United following a 2-2 draw at Anfield. Watched by a crowd of 38,858 fans, and in the Reds' second Charity Shield match, Bill Shankly's men led twice through Gordon Wallace and Gerry Byrne. But goals from Jonny Byrne and legendary striker Geoff Hurst six minutes from time decided the fate of the trophy.

TUESDAY 15th AUGUST 1972

Goals from John Toshack and Steve Heighway give Liverpool a 2-0 win over Manchester United at Anfield. It was the beginning of Toshack's third full season at Anfield after the Welshman's arrival from Cardiff City.

SUNDAY 16th AUGUST 1896

William E Barclay and John McKenna step down as Liverpool managers after spending four years and 127 games in charge of the club. It was McKenna who initially attempted to gain Liverpool admittance into the Football League in 1892, but the bid was rejected. After winning the Lancashire League that season, the club were finally given permission to join the Football League, winning their first game 2-0 at Middlesbrough Ironopolis. They have the highest win percentage of any managers in the club's history.

SATURDAY 16th AUGUST 1986

Ian Rush equalises with just two minutes to spare as Liverpool and Everton share the Charity Shield. It was the tenth time Liverpool had won the trophy, and the fourth time they had shared it, as both clubs kept the Shield for six months. Adrian Heath looked like he had given the Toffees the win when he netted with ten minutes left to play. But Liverpool's infamous never-say-die attitude shone through and Rush got his reward.

MONDAY 17th AUGUST 1964

Liverpool play in Europe for the first time and make their mark in style, beating Icelandic side Reykjavik 5-0 in the first leg of the European Cup first round. Gordon Wallace makes history when he scores the Reds' first goal in European competition after just three minutes and he adds a second later in the game. Roger Hunt also nets twice with Phil Chisnall scoring the other. Liverpool win the return leg at Anfield 6-1 to go through 11-1 on aggregate – not a bad start and a taste of what was to come in the future.

SATURDAY 18th AUGUST 1990

John Barnes equalises from the penalty spot six minutes after the interval as Liverpool and Manchester United share the Charity Shield for the third time after previously drawing in 1965 and 1977. Northern Ireland international Norman Whiteside had put Sir Alex Ferguson's team ahead just before half-time, but Barnes' equaliser ensures Liverpool's name is on the Shield for a record 13th time, at Wembley Stadium.

SATURDAY 19th AUGUST 2000

Garry McAllister becomes the Reds' oldest post-war debutant when he starts his Liverpool career against Bradford City. Aged 35 years and 237 days, McAllister makes a winning start at Anfield with Emile Heskey's 66th-minute goal enough to beat the Bantams.

SATURDAY 20th AUGUST 1983

Bryan Robson scores twice as FA Cup winners Manchester United win the Charity Shield, beating Division One champions Liverpool 2-0 at Wembley Stadium. It was only the third time Liverpool had lost in the competition, having won the Shield nine times previously. The game saw the introduction of a new Liverpool manager in a major final, after Joe Fagan was appointed on July 1st, following the retirement of Bob Paisley.

SATURDAY 20th AUGUST 1988

John Aldridge made up for his penalty miss in the previous campaign's FA Cup Final by scoring twice to win the Charity Shield for Liverpool. Although it was only small revenge having missed out on the more important trophy last season, it still left a sweet taste in the mouths of the travelling Liverpool fans who made the trip to Wembley Stadium to see their team win the Shield for the 11th time, the seventh time as outright winners. John Fashanu scored for Wimbledon as the game finished 2-1.

SATURDAY 20th AUGUST 2011

Arsenal's Aaron Ramsey puts through his own goal and Luis Suarez adds a late second as Liverpool finish strongly to beat Arsenal 2-0 at the Emirates Stadium. It's the Reds' first win away to the Gunners in 11 years and a first-ever victory at their new north London home.

SATURDAY 21st AUGUST 1982

Ian Rush scores the only goal of the game as Liverpool beat Tottenham Hotspur 1-0 to win the Charity Shield for the ninth time, the sixth time as outright winners. Spurs had beaten Queens Park Rangers 1-0 in the FA Cup Final replay in the previous campaign. The north London club competed in the previous campaign's Shield, which they drew 2-2 with Aston Villa.

SATURDAY 22nd AUGUST 1964

Match of the Day hits the screens for the first time on the BBC and Anfield is the chosen location for Liverpool's clash with Arsenal. The watching millions aren't disappointed, either, as the Reds record an opening-day 3-2 win over the Gunners.

MONDAY 22nd AUGUST 2011

Reds defender Sotirios Kyrgiakos joins Wolfsburg after finding first-team opportunities limited under Kenny Dalglish. The big Greek defender never gave less than his all during his time at Anfield and though he was never a regular starter, the £2m signing from AEK Athens won the respect of the supporters with his wholehearted displays. Kyrgiakos played 49 times in three years and scored three goals.

WEDNESDAY 23rd AUGUST 1972

Quick-fire first-half goals by John Toshack and Ian Callaghan are enough to beat Chelsea 2-1 at Stamford Bridge, maintaining the Reds' unbeaten start to the 1972/73 campaign.

FRIDAY 24th AUGUST 2001

Liverpool almost let a three-goal lead slip as European champions Bayern Munich mount a second-half rally in the Super Cup. But, the Reds hold out to win 3-2 following goals from John Arne Riise, Emile Heskey and Michael Owen.

WEDNESDAY 24th AUGUST 2011

Luis Suarez, Maxi Rodriguez and Andy Carroll all score as Liverpool ease past Exeter City in the Carling Cup second round. With more than 8,000 inside St James' Park, the Grecians never really threaten a cup upset, despite Danny Nardiello's late penalty.

SATURDAY 25th AUGUST 1993

The Reds see their 100% start to the 1993/94 season end as Tottenham Hotspur record only their third win in 48 visits to Anfield. Nigel Clough opens the scoring for the hosts who had won their opening three matches. Teddy Sheringham levels from the penalty spot on 30 minutes, and drives home the winner on 78 minutes, to give manager Ossie Ardiles a rare success against the Reds.

IAN CALLAGHAN, THE REDS' RECORD APPEARANCE MAKER (SEE 23RD AUGUST 1972).

FRIDAY 26th AUGUST 2005

Djibril Cisse is the hero for Liverpool as he scores a late equaliser and the extra-time winner in the Uefa Super Cup. Daniel Carvalho had given CSKA Moscow the lead just before the half-hour mark, and the Uefa Cup winners – and first Russian side to win a major European trophy – were on course for victory before Frenchman Cisse scored with eight minutes remaining. The former Auxerre striker, who cost Liverpool £14m, scored what proved to be the winner before Luis Garcia made it 3-1 with four minutes of the second period played at the Stade Louis II in Monaco.

SATURDAY 26th AUGUST 1967

Tony Hateley scores a hat-trick as Liverpool thrash Newcastle United 6-0 at Anfield. The centre forward had signed for the Reds from Chelsea for £96,000 in the summer, and these were his first goals for the club. Roger Hunt scored twice for Liverpool, who had made a good start to the season under Bill Shankly, and Emlyn Hughes got the other, which was the midfielder's first goal for the club in his second season.

SATURDAY 27th AUGUST 1932

Edmund Crawford made his Liverpool debut – and got on the score-sheet as Liverpool eased to victory over Wolverhampton Wanderers. The striker also rounded off the scoring with his second of the game as Liverpool went on to win 5-1. Gordon Hodgson got the Reds' first goal, before Dave Wright added another just two minutes later on the half hour mark. Crawford got his first three minutes before the interval and Gordon Gunson put the game beyond doubt just after the hour mark. Crawford sealed a fantastic debut, and ensured George Patterson left Anfield a happy man.

SATURDAY 28th AUGUST 1994

Arsenal had no reply to the Reds or rookie striker Robbie Fowler, who rifled in a hat-trick in just four minutes and 33 seconds in his first full season at Anfield. Fowler ended the campaign with 25 Premier League goals, second only to Blackburn's Alan Shearer – and he put another three past the Gunners the following year, too!

SATURDAY 29th AUGUST 1981

Bruce Grobbelaar, Craig Johnston and Mark Lawrenson all make their Liverpool debuts as Bob Paisley's team succumb to defeat at the hands of Wolverhampton Wanderers. Johnston came on as a second-half substitute for Ray Kennedy, but was unable to help the team's cause as they lost 1-0 at Molineux. Johnston went on to make 271 appearances for Liverpool and Lawrenson made 356, while Grobbelaar made 628 appearances in a glittering Anfield career.

SATURDAY 30th AUGUST 1919

Harry Chambers, Albert Pearson and Harry Lewis all score on their Liverpool debuts in a 3-1 victory over Bradford City. William Jenkinson also made his debut, but, as he played in defence, he was unable to add his name to the list of debut scorers on an incredible day for the Reds at Valley Parade. Lewis also missed a penalty, but it was still a fantastic day for the club and manager David Ashworth, who guided his team to a fourth-place finish at the end of the campaign.

WEDNESDAY 31st AUGUST 1960

Billy Liddell makes his last appearance for the club in an Anfield career spanning more than 14 years. The legendary winger played 534 times for Liverpool and scored 228 goals, but only managed to get his hands on one piece of silverware during his time with the club – the Division One title in 1946/47, ironically his first season. The Scotsman was signed from Lochgelly Violet as a 17-year-old and made his debut on January 5th 1940, when he scored the opening goal in a 2-0 victory over Chester City in an FA Cup third-round tie at Sealand Road. His last appearance unfortunately ended in defeat as Southampton won 1-0 at Anfield.

SATURDAY 31st AUGUST 1974

Ray Kennedy scores on his Liverpool debut as the Reds beat Chelsea 3-0 at Stamford Bridge. Kennedy joined the Reds from Arsenal and was the last piece of business Bill Shankly made before he retired as boss. It was an inspired move with Kennedy becoming an integral part of the all-conquering Liverpool team of the mid-1970s and early 1980s.

WEDNESDAY 31st AUGUST 1976

Ron Atkinson's West Bromwich Albion earn a creditable draw at Anfield with Ian Callaghan's 27th-minute goal earning the Reds a replay at The Hawthorns. The Baggies finished the job on their own patch winning 1-0, though Bob Paisley's men would learn from the lesson and go all the way to the final the season after, losing to Nottingham Forest in the replayed final after a 0-0 draw at Wembley.

WEDNESDAY 31st AUGUST 1983

Graeme Souness strikes home a 29th-minute winner to give Liverpool a 1-0 win over Norwich City at Carrow Road. The victory is the perfect riposte to the Canaries' league double over the Reds the season before with the East Anglian side inflicting the champions' only home league loss of the 1982/83 campaign.

SATURDAY 31st AUGUST 1985

West Ham United recover from a goal down to almost inflict the Reds' second defeat of the 1985/86 campaign. Frank McAvennie gives the Hammers a first-half lead before Craig Johnston levels on 52 minutes but McAvennie scores his second on 73 minutes to seemingly give the hosts all three points. Ronnie Whelan, however, has other ideas and the Republic of Ireland midfielder equalises with an 83rd-minute goal.

SATURDAY 31st AUGUST 1991

David Burrows ends his long wait for a Liverpool goal by scoring in the first minute of the 145th Merseyside derby against Everton. Dean Saunders and Ray Houghton are also on target as the Reds beat the Blues 3-1 at Anfield – a fifth successive win over the Toffees – in what is the last game between the teams before the Premiership begins the following season.

SATURDAY 31st AUGUST 1994

John Barnes rides some rough treatment from Southampton fans at The Dell to help inspire the Reds to a 2-0 win and maintain their 100% start to the season. Robbie Fowler nets his fifth in three games on 21 minutes, and Barnes makes it 2-0 on 78 minutes, to seal a satisfying victory for Liverpool.

LIVERPOOL FC
On This Day

SEPTEMBER

TUESDAY 1st SEPTEMBER 1896

Tom Watson, the club's longest-serving manager, takes charge of his first game. His side come away with maximum points as they beat Sheffield Wednesday 2-1. Having gained promotion to the top tier the previous season, Watson arrived at Liverpool in 1896 to replace management duo William Barclay and John McKenna. Watson had already won three league championships during his time at Sunderland and continues this success at Anfield. The popular manager spends almost two decades with the Reds and leads the club to their first league title in 1901. He repeats the feat in 1906 and helps the club reach their first-ever FA Cup Final in 1914, before sadly passing away one year later during his 19th season with the club.

SATURDAY 2nd SEPTEMBER 1893

The club win their first-ever league game away to Middlesbrough Ironopolis. Scottish winger Malcolm McVean scores the Reds' first league goal to lead his side to a 2-0 win. It's the first of 22 victories that season as the Anfield club go unbeaten throughout the campaign and ultimately claim promotion at the first attempt with a 2-0 Test match win over Newton Heath – soon to become arch-rivals Manchester United.

SATURDAY 2nd SEPTEMBER 1972

The Reds lose their second successive game in the East Midlands as Derby County come from behind to win 2-1 at The Baseball Ground. John Toshack's 16th-minute goal gives Liverpool the lead but the Rams, just like Leicester three days earlier, recover to take both points.

SATURDAY 3rd SEPTEMBER 1892

In front of 200 watching supporters, Liverpool win their first-ever competitive game with an 8-0 drubbing of Higher Walton. Opening their inaugural Lancashire League campaign, braces from John Smith, Jonathan Cameron and Joe McQue are added to goals from James McBride and Malcolm McVean to complete a sensational performance from 'the team of the Macs' – nicknamed because of the large number of Scottish players in that side with the 'Mc' prefix in their name. The result sets the standard for the rest of the season as Liverpool are crowned champions and invited to join the Football League following the 1892/93 campaign.

SATURDAY 4th SEPTEMBER 2010

Jamie Carragher scores for both Liverpool and Everton in his testimonial in front of 35,361 spectators at Anfield. The Liverpool line-up included 2005 Champions League winners Jerzy Dudek, Steve Finnan, Luis Garcia and Steven Gerrard, while Michael Owen and Gary McAllister also made an appearance in Liverpool's 4-1 victory. Garcia opened the scoring after two minutes before Carragher kept his composure from the spot to make it 2-0 with one minute of the first half remaining. Joe Cole added a third before Carragher scored a penalty for Everton, getting to the ball ahead of Yakubu to slot past the bemused Brad Jones. Nathan Eccleston completed the scoring with 20 minutes left to play as Carragher's boyhood team were ultimately brushed aside.

SATURDAY 5th SEPTEMBER 1953

Liverpool fans are forced to endure a 5-1 thrashing by Preston North End in what will eventually be the relegation season of 1953/54. Despite fielding a side that boasts club legend and future manager Bob Paisley, the Reds are shown up on home turf with only a second-half consolation goal from Billy Jones to show for their troubles. The loss comes just six games into the season but is indicative of the early form as the club win just one of their opening nine fixtures. With just nine wins to their name all season, the Preston result proves a sign of things to come as the club are relegated from the top tier for the first time in almost 50 years – it would take the club eight years to return to Division One.

SATURDAY 6th SEPTEMBER 1902

Having made his name as an Everton 'legend', Edgar Chadwick debuts for Liverpool. Alongside fellow debutant George Livingstone, Chadwick helps lead his side to a convincing 5-2 win over Blackburn Rovers at the start of a season where they go on to finish fifth. Prior to moving to Anfield, the inside-left had starred for the Reds' Merseyside rivals, scoring 97 goals in 270 appearances. His arrival at Anfield comes just three years after leaving Everton and despite reaching the latter part of his career during his time in the Red half of Liverpool, Edgar makes 43 appearances for the club but leaves in 1904 after the club suffers relegation.

SATURDAY 7th SEPTEMBER 1935

In the 69th meeting between the two sides, the club beats Everton 6-0 in the Reds' highest-scoring win over their arch-rivals. The win is Liverpool's first of the season and proves vital as the club struggles throughout the remainder of the season and finishes just three points off the relegation zone. Forward Fred Howe opens the scoring in the 15th minute, before Gordon Hodgson adds a brace and Howe doubles his own scoring tally, all before half-time. Four goals to the good, a 46,000-strong crowd are in good voice and celebrating a derby day win after just 45 minutes. The Reds continue their stellar performance in the second half, but must wait until the dying moments of the game to add to their goal tally as Howe completes his hat-trick in the 86th minute and adds a fourth three minutes later.

SATURDAY 8th SEPTEMBER 1906

Jack Cox scores Liverpool's only goal against Blackburn Rovers in a 1-1 draw at Ewood Park. Cox scored against Rovers almost 12 months to the day the previous season in a 3-1 defeat at Anfield and he will score a total of 80 goals in 360 appearances for the Reds during his time with the club.

SATURDAY 8th SEPTEMBER 2001

Jerzy Dudek makes his debut for the club but concedes three as the Reds are beaten 3-1 by Aston Villa. The Polish goalkeeper replaces Sander Westerveld as the club's new number one and impresses enough throughout his first season at the club to be nominated for the Uefa Goalkeeper of the Year award alongside Oliver Kahn and Gianluigi Buffon. The erratic goalkeeper proves an integral member of the squad during the six years he spends at Anfield and almost single-handedly wins his side the League Cup in 2003 with a Man of the Match performance in the final. A member of the 2005 Champions League-winning side and the triumphant 2006 FA Cup-winning side, Dudek's debut, despite ending in loss, begins six years of success for both club and player and he remains highly thought of by the Liverpool faithful.

JERZY DUDEK – ERRATIC BUT MUCH-LOVED FORMER KEEPER (SEE 8TH SEPTEMBER 2001).

WEDNESDAY 9th SEPTEMBER 1959

Roger Hunt caps his debut for the club with a goal against Scunthorpe United. The popular striker's second-half goal doubles Liverpool's lead during this Second Division fixture and the Reds run out 2-0 winners. It's the first of 245 league goals that Hunt goes on to score – a tally that makes him the highest league goalscorer in the club's history. Hunt becomes a crucial figure for the club during that era and scores goals that not only lead Liverpool to promotion in 1962, but also to two league championships, an FA Cup and a League Cup during the years that follow. During the 1961/62 campaign, Hunt scores 41 goals in 41 appearances – one of eight straight seasons that the forward would be named the club's top goalscorer. A winner of the 1966 World Cup during his time at Liverpool, his influence during his 11 years at Anfield would prove invaluable.

WEDNESDAY 10th SEPTEMBER 1930

During a season of high-scoring encounters, Liverpool beat Bolton Wanderers 7-2. Just nine days after suffering a 7-0 demolition at the hands of West Ham United, goals from Archie McPhearson (2), Dick Edmed (2), Gordon Hodgson (2) and Jimmy Smith make amends in exceptional style. The high goal count would continue throughout the season as the Reds beat Sheffield United 6-1 in November of the same year, only to lose 6-5 at Sunderland one week later!

SATURDAY 11th SEPTEMBER 1965

Chris Lawler and Roger Hunt are on target as Liverpool beat Fulham 2-1 at Anfield to maintain the Reds' 100% home record. More than 46,000 watch Bill Shankly's side ultimately cling on for a point after a spirited show by the Cottagers.

SATURDAY 11th SEPTEMBER 1999

Club favourite Sami Hyypia scores his first goal for the club and it comes against old enemies Manchester United. The Finn scores 22 goals from defence during his decade at Anfield and the Reds' reliable centre-back pops up with a 23rd-minute header in this fixture, but is undone by a duo of own goals by defensive partner Jamie Carragher as Liverpool lose 3-2.

THURSDAY 12th SEPTEMBER 1946

Albert Stubbins arrives from Newcastle United for a then club-record transfer fee. The centre forward, whose early career had been largely disrupted by the outbreak of World War II, is approached by both Liverpool and Merseyside rivals Everton and is reported to have made his choice by the flip of a coin. His signature costs Liverpool £12,500 but he instantly rewards that faith by scoring 28 goals during his first season and leading the club to their first league championship in 24 years. He goes on to score 75 goals in 159 appearances before retiring through injury in 1953.

WEDNESDAY 13th SEPTEMBER 1989

John Aldridge leaves the club after spending two years at Anfield and scoring 50 league goals. Having arrived as a long-term replacement for the outgoing Ian Rush in 1987, ironically it is Rush's return from Juventus one year later that ultimately brings an end to his time at the club. Though he appears in the same side as Rush during the 1988/89 season, as the Welsh favourite settles back in at Anfield, manager Kenny Dalglish eventually reverts to the partnership of Rush and Peter Beardsley, thus deeming Aldridge surplus to requirements. He throws his shirt and boots into the crowd after his final appearance for the Reds and becomes the first non-Basque player to join Real Sociedad.

SATURDAY 14th SEPTEMBER 1985

Kenny Dalglish's first signing as Liverpool manager, Steve McMahon, makes his debut for the club. Having arrived at the club from Aston Villa just two days earlier, McMahon appears for the first time in a 2-2 draw with Oxford United. Despite Alan Kennedy's own goal, Ian Rush and Craig Johnston find the net and earn the Reds a point during McMahon's first game of his six-year spell with the club, in which he wins three league championships and two FA Cups, before moving on to Manchester City in 1991.

WEDNESDAY 15th SEPTEMBER 1965

Geoff Strong becomes Liverpool's first-ever substitute when he replaces Chris Lawler in the home clash with West Ham United. His fresh legs prove vital, too, as Strong grabs a 76th-minute equaliser to earn a 1-1 draw.

WEDNESDAY 16th SEPTEMBER 1992

Ian Rush smashes Roger Hunt's Euro goal tally of 17 as he puts four past Cypriot side Apollon Limassol in the first leg of their European Cup Winners' Cup second-round tie. Paul Stewart's brace puts Graeme Souness' side two goals to the good, before Welsh talisman Rush begins his own goalscoring exploits with his side's third before half-time. Rush completes a majestic display with three more after the interval that take his goal tally in European competitions to 19 and sees his side qualify for an ultimately disappointing second-round tie with Spartak Moscow.

TUESDAY 17th SEPTEMBER 1974

A record-breaking performance by the Reds. Liverpool put on a show for a delighted Anfield crowd to ultimately render the second leg of their first-round European Cup Winners' Cup tie a dead rubber. Nine different players get their names on the score-sheet as Liverpool trounce Norwegian side Stromgodset 11-0 in this simply dominant display of football that brought about the highest scoring win in the club's history.

WEDNESDAY 18th SEPTEMBER 1991

Liverpool return from European exile in style with a 6-1 win over Kuusysi Lahti. Following the Heysel Stadium disaster of 1985, the Reds' return to European football is long overdue and they put in a stylish performance to mark their first Uefa Cup game in six years. Two from Ray Houghton and a second-half masterclass from Dean Saunders – who bags four - see the Finnish well and truly beaten. The Reds' own European journey eventually comes to an end following a quarter-final meeting with Italian side Genoa.

MONDAY 19th SEPTEMBER 1910

Club legend Ephraim Longworth makes the first of his 370 appearances for the club, but is unable to prevent his side slipping to a 2-0 defeat at the hands of Sheffield United. Despite an underwhelming debut, Longworth goes on to make nearly 400 appearances and in the process becomes one of the club's all-time greats. Remembered fondly both as a two-time league champion, and the club's first-ever England captain, Longworth finally hangs up his boots at the age of 40, having etched his name into the club's history forever.

DEAN SAUNDERS — ANOTHER IN A LONG LINE OF GREAT WELSH STRIKERS AT ANFIELD (SEE 18TH SEPTEMBER 1991).

WEDNESDAY 20th SEPTEMBER 2006

Xabi Alonso scores one of the most spectacular goals ever in the Premier League with a 70-yard strike against Newcastle United. Spotting Steve Harper off his line, the Spanish midfielder takes a punt from well within his own half and finds the back of the net to the delight of a flabbergasted Anfield crowd. At 70 yards, his goal is recognised as the longest-distance effort in Premier League history.

SATURDAY 21st SEPTEMBER 1985

Newly-appointed player-boss Kenny Dalglish scores after just 20 seconds of the 1985/86 Merseyside derby at Goodison Park. New signing Steve McMahon adds another after 16 minutes and Ian Rush puts the Reds 3-0 up, though goals from Graeme Sharp and Gary Lineker have the travelling Liverpool fans biting their nails towards the end of this thrilling encounter.

WEDNESDAY 22nd SEPTEMBER 1993

Legendary striker Robbie Fowler begins his 14-year-long love affair with the club by making his debut against Fulham in the League Cup. Already ahead, and with just minutes remaining, Liverpool's night is made complete as debutant Fowler caps his first appearance for the club with the first of his 183 goals. Despite leaving for Leeds in 2001, the twice PFA Young Player of the Year returns five years later and is welcomed back as a hero despite reaching the twilight of his career during his second spell at Anfield.

TUESDAY 23rd SEPTEMBER 1986

Steve McMahon scores four and can even afford to miss a penalty as his Liverpool side trounce Fulham 10-0 in the first leg of a League Cup second-round tie. Ian Rush (2), John Wark (2), Ronnie Whelan and Steve Nicol all score against the Cottagers.

WEDNESDAY 24th SEPTEMBER 1969

Phil Boersma becomes Liverpool's first League Cup substitute when he replaces Alun Evans in the 3-2 third-round defeat at Manchester City. Ronnie Evans and Bobby Graham's goals are not enough to prevent a City win at Maine Road – though at least the Reds can take comfort from seeing the Blues go on to win the competition!

SATURDAY 24th SEPTEMBER 1983

Phil Neal makes his 417th consecutive appearance for the Reds in a meeting with arch-rivals Manchester United, but his run is brought to an end when he is replaced in the 78th minute after suffering an injury. Having played in every game from 23rd October 1976 to the date of his injury, Neal holds the club record for consecutive appearances.

WEDNESDAY 25th SEPTEMBER 1968

Legendary England goalkeeper Ray Clemence makes his debut for the club in a 2-0 win over Swansea. Being carefully nurtured through the club's youth and reserve ranks, not until 1970 would Clemence establish himself as the club's first-choice goalkeeper. A five-time league champion and three-time European Cup winner, Clemence remains to this day one of the most decorated European goalkeepers in the history of football and shows early glimpses of promise during his first appearance in a Liverpool jersey by keeping a clean sheet against the Welsh opposition and helping his side reach the fourth round of the League Cup.

SATURDAY 26th SEPTEMBER 1931

Ted Savage scores two on debut for the Reds as Liverpool comfortably defeat Grimsby Town 4-0 at Anfield. Strangely, however, these two strikes prove to be Savage's only goals during his 105 appearances for the club and he eventually joins bitter rivals Manchester United during the 1937/38 campaign.

WEDNESDAY 27th SEPTEMBER 1978

In an all-English European Cup tie, Liverpool are eliminated from the competition by Nottingham Forest following a goalless draw at Anfield. Having been beaten 2-0 during the first leg of the tie, the Reds need a win at home to revive any hopes of progressing to the next round but are unable to fight back during the second leg, even failing to break to deadlock.

SUNDAY 28th SEPTEMBER 1884

Anfield hosts its first-ever game – but it is Everton and not Liverpool who act as hosts! Up against Earlestown, the Toffees win 5-0 at the ground that will soon become renowned around the world for playing host to their arch-rivals.

TUESDAY 29th SEPTEMBER 1981

The single most important, influential and most loved manager, Bill Shankly, dies aged 68. Shankly created two dynasties and dragged the club up by the scruff of its neck while changing the whole ethos of the Reds in the process. A manager who lived and breathed Liverpool Football Club from the moment he walked through the doors at Anfield, and a man who mapped out a successful blueprint that would ensure the Reds maintained a vice-like grip in England and in Europe. If ever a club and manager were meant for each other it is Liverpool and Bill Shankly – a legend in every sense imaginable and his 15 years as boss made the club the force it is today.

SATURDAY 29th SEPTEMBER 1984

Sheffield Wednesday ensure Liverpool's miserable start to the 1984/85 season continues with a 2-0 victory at Anfield. With just two wins from eight games, Joe Fagan's men will rely on a strong finish to the campaign to claim the runners-up spot.

SATURDAY 30th SEPTEMBER 1972

Larry Lloyd's goal on 40 minutes ends a 488-minute goal drought against Leeds United as Liverpool send a message to the rest of Division One with a stunning 2-1 victory at Elland Road. Goals from Lloyd and Phil Boersma silence the majority of the 46,468 crowd and the win is sweet revenge for the Reds who lost three times to the Lilywhites the season before, failing to score a single goal in four league and FA Cup matches with Don Revie's men.

WEDNESDAY 30th SEPTEMBER 1981

Just one day after the passing of Bill Shankly, a new club legend is born as Ian Rush scores his first-ever goal for the club. One year after joining, the Welsh wonder finally breaks his duck during the 7-0 thrashing of Oulun Palloseura in the European Cup. Entering the fray just three minutes earlier, Rush adds his name to the score-sheet in the 67th minute, though few could have known a further 138 league goals would follow during Rush's first spell at the club, nor that he would add another 90 to his league tally upon his return to Anfield following a stint with Juventus.

LIVERPOOL FC
On This Day

OCTOBER

WEDNESDAY 1st OCTOBER 1980

Two Liverpool players lay claim to the matchball as their side demolish Oulun Palloseura in the second leg, first round of the European Cup. Two from Graeme Souness set the Reds on their way to a 10-1 victory over their Finnish opposition, before Terry McDermott adds a brace of his own before half-time. Souness is the first to complete his hat-trick when Liverpool are awarded a penalty just seven minutes into the second half and Sammy Lee, Ray Kennedy and David Fairclough (2) all find the net before McDermott scores his third with 83 on the clock. Liverpool go on to claim the trophy with Souness and McDermott finishing joint top goalscorers with six each to their name.

SATURDAY 1st OCTOBER 1983

Sunderland earn a surprise three points at Anfield with a 1-0 victory over the Reds. Less than 30,000 attend the game as crowds around the country continue to decline and the home loss is one of two suffered during a difficult first half of the season.

WEDNESDAY 2nd OCTOBER 1968

A night of high-octane, but ultimately disappointing, drama on a memorable European night at Anfield as Liverpool, trailing 2-1 in the European Fairs Cup (a forerunner for the Uefa Cup) and 1-0 on the night, score two late goals to force the first-round tie into extra time. Chris Lawler and Emlyn Hughes both score in the last 15 minutes to send the near-50,000 home fans wild and make it 3-3 on aggregate, but with no more goals in extra time and no penalty shoot-outs at the time, the Reds then lose the overall match on the toss of a coin!

FRIDAY 2nd OCTOBER 1991

Left-back Barry Jones makes his one and only appearance for the Anfield club. Appearing in a Uefa Cup tie with Finnish minnows Kuusysi Lahti, Jones' debut ends in a 1-0 defeat, but Liverpool progress to the next round anyway having won the first leg 6-1. The defender goes on to make more than 250 appearances for Wrexham following his exit from Anfield.

WEDNESDAY 3rd OCTOBER 1973

Two goals in nine second-half minutes from an own goal, and John Toshack, hand Liverpool a 2-0 victory over Jeunesse d'Esch in the second leg of their European Cup first-round tie to win 3-1 overall. The plucky Luxembourg outfit had forced a surprise 1-1 draw in the first leg and the return at Anfield proves anything but a formality as the Reds eventually edge through to the second round of the competition.

SATURDAY 3rd OCTOBER 1981

Two Terry McDermott penalties prevent John Toshack enjoying a winning return to Anfield. The former Liverpool legend sees his talented Swansea side take a first-half lead but ultimately, the 2-2 draw the Welsh leave with is an excellent result. The Swans win the return fixture 2-0 at the Vetch Field later in the season – one of only three away defeats for Bob Paisley's men during the 1981/82 campaign.

SATURDAY 3rd OCTOBER 2010

Roy Hodgson's reign as Liverpool boss hits a new low with a 2-1 home defeat to Ian Holloway's Blackpool. Charlie Adam and Luke Varney give the Seasiders a 2-0 lead at the break before Kyrgiakos pulls one back eight minutes after the break. The Liverpool fans chant 'Dalglish!' before the final whistle goes, making their opinions clear...

SATURDAY 4th OCTOBER 1980

Howard Gayle becomes the first black player to ever represent the club. He replaces David Fairclough in the 69th minute of the Reds' 3-0 win over Manchester City and though he will go on to make just five appearances for the club, his performance in the second leg of the 1981 European Cup semi-final against Bayern Munich is still fondly remembered by fans of that era.

SATURDAY 4th OCTOBER 1998

Chelsea look like avenging their two previous visits to Anfield which resulted in 4-2 and 5-1 defeats as they lead 1-0 with moments to go courtesy of Pierluigi Casiraghi's tenth-minute goal. Jamie Redknapp, however, has different ideas and his free kick levels matters on 84 minutes.

TUESDAY 5th OCTOBER 1993

Robbie Fowler runs rings around the Fulham defence in the second round of the League Cup as he knocks five past the Cottagers. Single-handedly winning the game for his side, Fowler becomes only the fifth player to score five in one match for the Reds. Scoring two in the first 21 minutes, Fowler completes his hat-trick just two minutes after the interval and scores his fourth and fifth before the clock has even reached the 70 minute mark as the Reds run out 5-0 victors.

SUNDAY 5th OCTOBER 2010

Liverpool make a stunning comeback after going 2-0 down to Manchester City at the City of Manchester Stadium. The Reds had been outplayed during the first 45 minutes and goals from Stephen Ireland and Javier Garrido gave the hosts a deserved two-goal cushion, but Rafa's boys were far from finished. Fernando Torres reduced the arrears on 55 minutes – scoring Liverpool's 1,000th Premier League goal in the process – and then City's Pablo Zabaleta was sent off for a foul on Xabi Alonso. Torres then made it 2-2 on 72 minutes with his second of the afternoon before Dirk Kuyt's last-minute winner completed a fantastic comeback by the Reds.

SUNDAY 6th OCTOBER 1991

Just 48 hours after signing for his boyhood club, Rob Jones makes his debut for the Reds. Up against arch-rivals Manchester United, Jones helps his side keep a clean sheet in a goalless draw, but is replaced in the 65th minute after Gary Ablett is sent off and leaves Liverpool with just ten men. A winner of the 1992 FA Cup and 1995 League Cup, Jones takes no time at all to make an impression and is soon called up by England.

WEDNESDAY 7th OCTOBER 1981

Liverpool start their 1982 League Cup-winning campaign with a 5-0 drubbing of Exeter. Ian Rush (2), Kenny Dalglish, Ronnie Whelan and Terry McDermott all find the net, as the Reds make light work of their second-round opposition in front of an Anfield crowd who will go on to celebrate success in the competition that same season.

SATURDAY 8th OCTOBER 1949

Popular full-back Ray Lambert scores the first of his two goals for the club in a 2-0 win over Middlesbrough. Having gone in front through a 74th-minute Jimmy Payne goal, Lambert's side win a penalty just three minutes later and he is offered the chance to take it. Never having scored in his three years with the club, the pressure was clearly on for the fans' favourite to delight his faithful with a goal as he slots home. He would wait a further four years before scoring his second and final goal for the club!

TUESDAY 9th OCTOBER 1990

Ian Rush is at his magical best as he scores a hat-trick in a 4-1 win away at Crewe Alexandra. Steve Staunton scores Liverpool's only other goal of the game with a first-half strike to ensure his side lead at the interval and Rush completes his hat-trick in style with a second-half brace that leads Liverpool to the third round of the League Cup.

SATURDAY 10th OCTOBER 1953

A 6-1 win over Aston Villa proves a rare ray of light for Liverpool fans during the relegation season of 1953/54. A goal up at half-time thanks to Billy Liddell, the Reds took charge during the second half as Sammy Smyth (2), Bob Paisley and Jimmy Payne all add to an 88th-minute own goal to ensure victory. The club are unable to continue this good form throughout the rest of the season, however, eventually slipping into the second tier of English football.

SATURDAY 10th OCTOBER 1992

Bruce Grobbelaar misses a penalty in his own testimonial as Liverpool draw 2-2 with Everton at Anfield. Don Hutchison and Steve McManaman were amongst those who made an appearance for the South African, who spent 13 years at the club. During his tenure he won a host of trophies, including six Division One titles (three in consecutive seasons between 1981 and 1984) and a European Cup after beating Roma on penalties in Rome. David Burrows and Ronny Rosenthal scored the goals for Liverpool in front of 20,514 fans.

SUNDAY 10th OCTOBER 1993

Guest player Maurice Johnston scores Liverpool's only goal in Steve Nicol's testimonial against a Great Britain XI at Anfield in front of just over 12,000 fans. Nicol was an integral part of the club's dominance in the 1980s after he signed from Ayr for £300,000. He featured in 468 games during his Liverpool career, scoring 46 goals, including a rare hat-trick against Newcastle at St James' Park on September 20th 1987. Sammy Lee and Alan Hansen also played for Liverpool in Nicol's testimonial.

SATURDAY 11th OCTOBER 1902

Oldham-born Peter Platt makes his debut for the club. The young goalkeeper appears for the Reds on their visit to the Hawthorns and despite conceding a goal, his side beat West Bromwich Albion 2-1. Not until the end of the 1902/03 season does Platt eventually establish himself as the club's first choice. His reign as the club's number one doesn't last long, however, as he is replaced halfway through the following campaign by Charles Cotton.

SATURDAY 12th OCTOBER 1895

In the first-ever meeting between the Reds and soon-to-be bitter rivals Newton Heath (Manchester United), Liverpool run out 7-1 winners to claim first blood in what would become one of the greatest rivalries in European football. Frank Becton, Thomas Bradshaw and Fred Greary grab a brace each, but all are unable to complete their hat-tricks, before Jimmy Ross adds a seventh with just minutes remaining. Though United would make amends with a 5-2 win in the reverse fixture, Liverpool win promotion as Division Two champions that year, with their rivals finishing a long way off in sixth.

SATURDAY 12th OCTOBER 1968

Goals from Ian St John and Alun Evans send more than 53,000 fans wild as Liverpool beat Manchester United 2-0. It's the Reds' sixth win in seven games and the victory sends a message to the rest of Division One that Bill Shankly's team are a force to be reckoned with. Despite losing the next game 2-1, Liverpool then repeat this run with another six wins and a draw in their next seven games.

STEVE NICOL – ENJOYED A LONG AND DISTINGUISHED CAREER FOR THE REDS (SEE 10TH OCTOBER 1993).

SATURDAY 13th OCTOBER 1894

Meeting in the first-ever top-flight Merseyside derby, Liverpool are beaten 3-0 by local rivals Everton. In front of a 44,000-strong Goodison Park crowd, the Reds can do nothing to prevent the Toffees walking away with maximum points during a season when good results prove hard to come by. So hard, in fact, that the club eventually suffer relegation back to the Second Division at the end of the campaign, having only been promoted to the top tier during the previous season.

SATURDAY 14th OCTOBER 1972

Chris Lawler's 40th-minute goal gives Liverpool a vital 1-0 lead over Southampton at The Dell, but the Saints level after the break to earn a deserved 1-1 draw.

SATURDAY 14th OCTOBER 1978

Liverpool thrash Derby County 5-0 at Anfield during the championship-winning season of 1978/79. David Johnson puts the Reds in front just before the half-hour mark to ensure his side are in front at the interval. Ray Kennedy and Kenny Dalglish both score twice to provide further evidence that the Reds are the team to stop in a season that the club goes on to dominate. Never off the top of the table having reached the summit after just the second game of the campaign, Liverpool also beat Spurs 7-0 and Norwich 6-0 on their way to the Division One crown.

SATURDAY 15th OCTOBER 1994

Former Anfield legend Kenny Dalglish records a third straight victory over Liverpool as Blackburn edge a five-goal thriller at Ewood Park. Robbie Fowler gives the Reds the lead before Mark Atkins and Chris Sutton put Rovers 2-1 up. John Barnes makes it 2-2 before the hour mark but Sutton has the last laugh to give Rovers a 3-2 win and maintain their 100% home record.

WEDNESDAY 15th OCTOBER 2005

Djibril Cisse knocks home a winner 15 minutes from time to give Liverpool a 1-0 victory over Blackburn Rovers at Anfield.

FRIDAY 15th OCTOBER 2010

New England Sports Ventures completes its takeover of the club. Following a period of great instability and unrest under the ownership of American businessmen Tom Hicks and George Gillett, the club is sold to fellow American John W Henry. Though Hicks and Gillett had supported the club financially during their time in charge, reported conflict between the two men meant for a difficult working environment and the struggles behind the scenes soon took their toll on the pitch as Liverpool's status as one of the Premier League's 'big four' came under threat. NESV had courted the club for a number of months and after weeks of speculation, the takeover is finally completed. Soon replacing manager Roy Hodgson with former boss and club legend Kenny Dalglish, the club's new owners fund big money moves for Andy Carroll, Luis Suarez and Jordan Henderson as the Reds work hard to repair some of the damage done under the previous regime. Going into the 2011/12 campaign, the general feeling among Liverpool fans is, 'so far, so good'.

MONDAY 16th OCTOBER 1899

Prolific Reds striker George Allan is robbed of the opportunity to reach the very top of the game as he dies of tuberculosis, aged just 24. Having scored 41 goals in 49 games during his first spell at the club, the Scottish centre forward joins Celtic in 1897 but despite scoring 15 in 17 for the Scots, he lasts just one year north of the border before returning to Anfield in 1898. However, Allan contracts a deadly illness and is forced to retire from the game, eventually passing away in 1899.

SATURDAY 17th OCTOBER 1987

Striker John Aldridge scores in his tenth consecutive league game as he converts from the spot against QPR. Aldridge's goal is one of four that day as Craig Johnston, and a brace from John Barnes, contributes to the 4-0 drubbing of the London side. But, the game is best remembered for the Irishman's penalty that set the club record for consecutive league goals.

MONDAY 17th OCTOBER 1994

Robbie Fowler and Lee Jones score the goals for Liverpool, who beat Brighton & Hove Albion 2-1 at the Goldstone Ground in Jimmy Case's testimonial. Case was one of the toughest midfielders of his time and, during his Liverpool career, scored 46 goals in 269 appearances for the club during the 1970s when trophies were flooding in. He moved to the Albion in 1981 when he was used as a makeweight in Liverpool's signing of Mark Lawrenson.

SUNDAY 18th OCTOBER 1992

Liverpool legend Ian Rush smashes the club goalscoring record with a strike against Manchester United. Though Rush's side are denied victory at Old Trafford by United's Mark Hughes, goals from Don Hutchison and Rush ensure the Reds come away with a point as the Welsh striker scores his 287th goal for the club – surpassing the record set by fellow great Roger Hunt.

WEDNESDAY 19th OCTOBER 1977

The Reds hammer Dynamo Dresden 5-1 on their way to 1978 European Cup success. Alan Hansen scores his debut goal for the club after just 14 minutes, before Jimmy Case and Phil Neal put Liverpool three goals to the good at half-time. Case added his second after the interval and Ray Kennedy completed the scoring with more than 20 minutes remaining. Though the German side win the return leg on home soil, Liverpool progress through to the third round with ease and go on to defeat Belgian side Club Brugge in the final of the competition to lift the trophy for a fourth time.

MONDAY 19th OCTOBER 1987

John Barnes scores twice as Liverpool beat Dundee 4-1 in a testimonial game for former Dees player George McGeachie. The Scotsman spent 13 seasons at Dens Park, where he helped Dundee to win the Scottish First Division in 1979. It was the only honour the Falkirk-born defender won in his long Dundee career, in which he made well over 200 appearances. Ray Houghton and Ronnie Whelan were also on the score-sheet for Liverpool on the night in front of 14,463 spectators.

FRIDAY 20th OCTOBER 1961

Club record scorer Ian Rush is born in Flint, Wales. The Welsh striker made his name for Chester City between 1978 and 1980, before moving to Anfield, aged 18, for £300,000. There had been much interest in the talented teenager – notably from Manchester City – and Bob Paisley's decision to sign Rush was eventually justified as he scored the first of his 229 league goals one year after joining. Following a disappointing stint in Italy with European giants Juventus, Rush returns to Anfield for a second spell, scoring a further 90 goals for the club. Though he eventually left for good in 1996, the striker is fondly remembered by Reds and remains to this day their all-time record goalscorer with 346 in all competitions.

TUESDAY 21st OCTOBER 1997

The Reds suffer an ultimately decisive 3-0 loss to Strasbourg in the first leg of their Uefa Cup second-round tie. Though Liverpool would win the return leg 2-0 at Anfield, Roy Evans' side were unable to recover the three-goal deficit as two from David Zitelli and one from Dennis Conteh condemn them to a surprise defeat.

SATURDAY 22nd OCTOBER 1983

Liverpool stalwart Steve Nicol scores his first goal for the club. The Scot finds the net with seven minutes remaining to beat Queens Park Rangers 1-0. The reliable defender goes on to score 45 more goals during his 13-year stint with the Anfield club and becomes Liverpool's longest-serving player (in terms of unbroken service). A winner of the Football Writers' Footballer of the Year award, Nicol makes 468 appearances for the club before making his last appearance for the Reds on this same date.

WEDNESDAY 23rd OCTOBER 1991

Jamie Redknapp makes his first appearance for the club in a Uefa Cup second-round tie against Auxerre. Having arrived as Kenny Dalglish's final signing, an 18-year-old Redknapp becomes the youngest player ever to represent the club in a European competition as he makes the first of his 308 appearances. Wearing the popular number seven shirt, Redknapp shows early glimpses of promise for Liverpool but is replaced after 79 minutes. The consummate professional goes on to appear for England during his 11 years at Anfield, before moving on to Tottenham Hotspur.

SATURDAY 24th OCTOBER 1998

Michael Owen puts four past a helpless Nottingham Forest as Liverpool pull off a sensational 5-1 win. A 23rd-minute Steve McManaman strike separates Owen's first-half double to put the Reds in a commanding position. The England international then steps up to score from the spot to complete his hat-trick in the 71st minute, before capping a stunning display with a fourth just six minutes later, to the delight of the Anfield faithful.

SUNDAY 25th OCTOBER 1995

The Reds outplay Norwich City to win 4-1 at Anfield. Though the Canaries go on to finish the season three places above Liverpool in third, goals from Michael Thomas, Don Hutchinson, David Burrows, and a Mark Walters penalty, provide the Anfield club with a convincing victory as Mark Bowen misses from the spot on a difficult day for the visitors.

THURSDAY 26th OCTOBER 1939

Twice-league champion Willie Stevenson is born in Edinburgh, Scotland. The Scottish left-half makes 241 appearances for Liverpool between 1962 and 1967, scoring 18 goals. A skilful and creative player, Stevenson becomes a winner of the FA Cup, and three Charity Shield medals, during his time at the club and also claims a European Cup Winners' Cup runners-up medal during his five-year stint on Merseyside.

SATURDAY 27th OCTOBER 1962

Tommy Lawrence makes his first appearance in a Liverpool goalkeeper jersey during a 1-0 loss to West Bromwich Albion. Though he's beaten on this day, Lawrence takes over as the club's number one and is the man between the sticks during the great Bill Shankly era. He makes 390 appearances during his 14 years at Anfield before eventually being replaced by the great Ray Clemence. The Scotland international's trophy cabinet is full of medals by the time he joins Tranmere Rovers in 1971, having won the league championship on two occasions, the Charity Shield on three and the FA Cup in 1965. His Liverpool side finish runners-up in the 1966 European Cup Winners' Cup and his superb form for the club meant that Clemence would have to wait two years before eventually establishing himself as the club's first choice.

TUESDAY 28th OCTOBER 1873

Frank Becton is born in Preston. Having impressed for his boyhood club, Becton moves on to Liverpool in 1895 for a fee of £100. Despite scoring 42 goals in 86 games, Becton leaves after three years and sadly dies aged just 36 after contracting tuberculosis.

SATURDAY 29th OCTOBER 1983

Ian Rush puts in a five-star performance during a 6-0 win over Luton Town. With two in the first five minutes, Rush was quick off the mark and completed his hat-trick after just 36 minutes. Kenny Dalglish makes it four before half-time but it is Rush who takes all the headlines as he adds two more to his tally after the interval. He is one of just five players to score five in one game for the club.

SATURDAY 30th OCTOBER 1920

The Reds travel to Goodison Park and overcome their rivals with a 3-0 win. Dick Johnson scores one, and Harry Chambers finds the net either side of half-time, to complete a comprehensive win in front of 55,000 devastated Toffees fans.

THURSDAY 31st OCTOBER 1996

In a high-scoring European Cup Winners' Cup clash, Liverpool run out 6-3 winners against Swiss side Sion. With the score at 2-1 from the first leg in Switzerland, Liverpool fall two goals behind after just 23 minutes, before Steve McManaman pulls one back for the Reds before half-time. Stig Bjornebye equalises for the Reds within ten minutes of the restart, before a spirited Sion retake the lead. John Barnes scores within minutes to draw level once again and his side go on to run riot as a Robbie Fowler double and a last-minute Patrick Berger strike send Liverpool through.

SATURDAY 31st OCTOBER 2009

A Halloween horror as the nine-men Reds go down 3-1 at Craven Cottage. Bobby Zamora puts Fulham ahead before Fernando Torres levels for Liverpool but Erik Nevland made it 2-1 before Philipp Degen and Jamie Carragher saw red within three minutes. Clint Dempsey sealed the points with a killer third on 87 minutes.

LIVERPOOL FC
On This Day

NOVEMBER

WEDNESDAY 1st NOVEMBER 2000

Robbie Fowler grabs an extra-time winner to send Liverpool through to the fourth round of the League Cup at Chelsea's expense. Danny Murphy had put the Reds ahead after 11 minutes but Gianfranco Zola levelled the scores after 29 minutes. Fowler's 104th-minute winner spares the near-30,000 crowd the lottery of penalties.

SATURDAY 2nd NOVEMBER 1963

Gerry and the Pacemakers' You'll Never Walk Alone reaches number one in the UK charts. This is the first week of four that it will spend in the top position. It has already become the club's unofficial anthem, and is repeatedly sung on the terraces at Anfield. Before every match, the opposition fans are treated to a rendition of the song. The famous 'Shankly Gates' are also adorned with the song's title as a reminder to all supporters.

TUESDAY 2nd NOVEMBER 1982

Finnish side HJK Helsinki are defeated 5-0 in the European Cup second round at Anfield. Left-back Alan Kennedy nets the final two goals, after Liverpool run into an unassailable 3-0 half-time lead thanks to strikes from forward, Kenny Dalglish. Australian Craig Johnston and Phil Neal get the others to make it a rout.

SATURDAY 2nd NOVEMBER 2002

Liverpool move seven points clear at the top of the Premier League after Michael Owen scores a goal in each half to see off a stubborn West Ham United. With the visitors looking for a first Anfield win since 1963, Owen bags a stunning double with strikes after 24 and 55 minutes to put Gerard Houllier's side well clear of nearest challengers Arsenal.

SATURDAY 3rd NOVEMBER 1956

Liverpool recover from a 4-1 defeat at Barnsley to thump struggling Port Vale by the same score. Despite going in 1-0 down at the break, the Reds score four after the interval, including a Johnny Wheeler four-minute hat-trick late on. Billy Liddell grabs the equaliser to set the ball rolling.

WEDNESDAY 3rd NOVEMBER 1976

Liverpool beat Trabzonspor 3-0 at Anfield to progress to the next round of the European Cup. The side are a goal behind going into the second leg, and are soon on level terms thanks to a goal from Steve Heighway. Strikes from David Johnson and Kevin Keegan confirm the team's advancement to the next stage.

SATURDAY 3rd NOVEMBER 1973

Liverpool end their appalling form on the road with an impressive 2-0 victory at Highbury. Having won all six of their games at Anfield, the Reds desperately needed success on the road to ignite their title challenge and late goals from Emlyn Hughes and John Toshack ended a run of eight away games without a victory.

SATURDAY 3rd NOVEMBER 1979

Liverpool shift through the gears in impressive style to destroy a more than useful Wolves side at Anfield. Kenny Dalglish scores twice and Ray Kennedy rounds off the goals in a 3-0 victory, watched by 48,128 fans.

SATURDAY 3rd NOVEMBER 1984

Ronnie Whelan's 86th-minute winner leaves Liverpool away from the relegation zone and into mid-table with a 1-0 away win over basement club Stoke City.

WEDNESDAY 3rd NOVEMBER 2004

Liverpool travel to northern Spain to take on Deportivo La Coruna, winning 1-0 in La Riazor. Rafa Benitez sends out a defensively-minded side, which won thanks to an own-goal from centre-back Jorge Andrade. The other moment of interest in the match is when Igor Biscan manages to knock out goalkeeper Chris Kirkland in the second period.

SATURDAY 4th NOVEMBER 1987

Ray Houghton's first Liverpool goal is enough to earn the Reds a draw away to Wimbledon. The Dons prove a tough nut to crack at Plough Lane and the Division One leaders have to be happy with a 1-1 draw in a bruising battle watched by 13,544 fans.

SUNDAY 4th NOVEMBER 2001

Anfield rocks as Liverpool beat Manchester United 3-1 to move within a point of leaders Leeds United. Michael Owen and John Arne Riise put the Reds 2-0 up at the break but David Beckham pulls one back for United on 51 minutes. Owen scores within a minute to restore the two-goal lead that earns all three points against Sir Alex Ferguson's side.

WEDNESDAY 4th NOVEMBER 2009

Ryan Babel scores the club's 550th goal in Europe by netting Liverpool's solitary strike in a Champions League group game against Lyon in France that ended with the sides sharing the points. Unfortunately, it was not enough for the Reds to progress from the first phase as they do not earn sufficient points to finish in the top two places.

THURSDAY 4th NOVEMBER 2010

Captain fantastic, Steven Gerrard hits a hat-trick as Liverpool down the Italian giants, Napoli, at Anfield in a Europa League group game. The club's talismanic captain had started the match on the bench, but came on at half-time, with the team from Naples leading by a single goal, to turn the game on its head. His first goal came in the 75th minute, before going on to net twice in the final moments of the game to give Liverpool a 3-1 win.

SATURDAY 5th NOVEMBER 2005

Liverpool defeat Aston Villa 2-0 away. Steven Gerrard scores the first goal on his 300th appearance for the club, before the unlikely figure of Xabi Alonso hits a rare strike, when his shot made its way through Villa's goalkeeper, Thomas Sorensen, to guarantee the points with only two minutes left on the clock.

SUNDAY 5th NOVEMBER 1911

Berry Nieuwenhuys is born in Boksburg, South Africa. He starts out as an engineer, playing football part-time. The midfielder signs for Liverpool in 1933, making his debut in September. Known for his pace and quick feet, Nieuwenhuys plays 239 league games for Liverpool, with his time at the club halted due to World War II. During his spell in England, he also represents the Hurst Hawks baseball team.

SATURDAY 6th NOVEMBER 1982

Ian Rush scored four as Liverpool hammered their local rivals Everton 5-0 in a Merseyside derby at Goodison Park. The home side were not aided by the sending off of Glenn Keeley when he dragged Kenny Dalglish back, with the striker through on goal. A Mark Lawrenson strike was sandwiched in between the Welshman's four goals, as Liverpool dominated the match throughout.

TUESDAY 6th NOVEMBER 2007

Liverpool earn their biggest Champions League win by defeating Besiktas 8-0 at Anfield. Yossi Benayoun hits his first hat-trick for Liverpool, as Peter Crouch and Ryan Babel both bag a brace with Steven Gerrard netting the other. It's a vital result for Liverpool having needed three points to keep their Champions League dreams alive.

TUESDAY 7th NOVEMBER 1967

Roger Hunt breaks the club's goalscoring record by netting his 242nd Liverpool goal, in the Inter-Cities Fairs Cup against TSV Munich, as the team smash eight. He leaves the club in 1969 to sign for Bolton Wanderers with 286 goals to his name. Hunt would maintain his record for another 23 years, until Ian Rush finally surpasses his tally.

SATURDAY 7th NOVEMBER 1992

Striker Ronny Rosenthal scores twice as Liverpool defeat Middlesbrough in a league game at Anfield. The final result is 4-1, thanks to the Israeli setting the home side on their way with two first-half goals. Youngster Steve McManaman got the third just before the interval, whilst Ian Rush completed the scoring in the final minute of the game, to get his 200th league goal for the club.

SATURDAY 8th NOVEMBER 1975

Liverpool get the better of Manchester United at Anfield. Their bitter rivals are not up to the task in front of 49,136 fans, as Liverpool run out 3-1 victors. Steve Heighway scored the first for the Reds, before Welshman John Toshack, and Kevin Keegan, get one goal each in the second period. The win puts Bob Paisley's men above United and just one point behind leaders West Ham United.

SATURDAY 8th NOVEMBER 1997

Liverpool demolish Spurs by scoring four goals without reply at Anfield. The first half ends goalless, but it only took two minutes of the second period for Liverpool to open the scoring when Steve McManaman nets the opener. Strikes from Oyvind Leonhardsen, Jamie Redknapp and Michael Owen would confirm the points for the home side in front of over 38,000 fans.

SATURDAY 9th NOVEMBER 1907

Liverpool defeat the country's oldest professional club 6-0 when Notts County are the unfortunate visitors to Anfield for this First Division clash. Striker Joe Hewitt hits three of the 79 goals he scored during his Liverpool career, whilst being ably assisted by Bill McPherson, Charles Hewitt and Robbie Robinson, netting a goal each.

WEDNESDAY 9th NOVEMBER 1994

Chelsea leave Anfield pointless, as Liverpool win 3-1. Two quick-fire goals from Robbie Fowler made the difference early on, as the striker nets twice within 90 seconds to set Liverpool on their way to victory. Neil Ruddock put the Reds out of sight, when he scored in the 25th minute to ensure the points stayed in the north-west.

SATURDAY 10th NOVEMBER 1984

Jim Beglin makes his Liverpool debut over a year after signing for the club for £20,000 from Shamrock Rovers. He starts on the left-hand side of midfield in a league game against Southampton. He eventually makes the left full-back role his own under the management of Kenny Dalglish, going on to play 98 league games for the club, before breaking his leg, costing him his place in the side.

SATURDAY 10th NOVEMBER 2007

Liverpool defeat Fulham 2-0 at Anfield. Like in many games, the team's two most pivotal players were at the forefront of everything that happened on the pitch; Fernando Torres and Steven Gerrard scored the two goals late in the game. Striker Torres netted just ten minutes after coming on to put Liverpool in the lead, before his captain converted a penalty.

WEDNESDAY 11th NOVEMBER 1970

Forward John Toshack arrives for a club record £110,000 from Cardiff City. He will stay at the club for the following eight years, winning eight major honours in the process. His most prolific spell was after Kevin Keegan arrived, as the pair struck up a nigh-on telepathic understanding. Toshack leaves for Swansea in 1978, going on to have an extremely successful managerial career, both in the UK and abroad.

WEDNESDAY 11th NOVEMBER 1992

Liverpool defeat Sheffield United in a League Cup third-round replay at Anfield in front of only 17,654 fans. Winger Steve McManaman scores twice in the first half to give Liverpool the upper hand on the South Yorkshire outfit. The win, and the Reds' progression, is confirmed with six minutes to go as Mike Marsh converts a penalty.

THURSDAY 12th NOVEMBER 1998

Roy Evans resigns after joint management with Gerard Houllier proves to be unsuccessful. Evans won 116 of his 226 games in charge of Liverpool, and guided the club to fourth place in the Premier League and to a League Cup triumph in his first full season at the helm, with young prodigy Steve McManaman getting both goals in a 2-1 victory over Bolton Wanderers. Evans is also responsible for the arrival of Michael Owen on the football scene, giving him an opportunity in his final campaign in charge.

TUESDAY 12th NOVEMBER 2002

Liverpool gain a point in a topsy-turvy Champions League group stage clash with Basel in Switzerland. The two teams shared the points in a six-goal thriller. All of Liverpool's goals came in the second half as Danny Murphy and Vladimir Smicer score within three minutes of each other, before Michael Owen hit home the rebound from a saved penalty.

SATURDAY 12th NOVEMBER 1977

Liverpool's poor run of form continues with a 2-0 defeat to lowly QPR at Loftus Road. It's a third successive loss for the Reds following defeats at Manchester City and at home to Aston Villa.

WEDNESDAY 13th NOVEMBER 1974

Terry McDermott signs from Newcastle United. The midfielder goes on to become an integral part of the club's engine room after two seasons of being on the fringes of the starting XI. In 1980 he wins the PFA Players' Player of the Year and Football Writers' awards, becoming the first player to receive both in the same year.

WEDNESDAY 13th NOVEMBER 1996

Liverpool thrash Charlton Athletic at Anfield in the League Cup. It takes a replay for the Reds to get the better of their lower league opposition, but Mark Wright and Jamie Redknapp's first-half goals give Liverpool a two-goal advantage with less than 20 minutes played. Robbie Fowler confirms Liverpool's progression late on by bagging a brace to make the result 4-1.

WEDNESDAY 14th NOVEMBER 1956

Avi Cohen is born in Cairo, Egypt. He joins Liverpool in 1979 for a fee of £200,000 from Maccabi Tel-Aviv, becoming the first Israeli to play in England. Unfortunately, he is never able to get a run in the team, and is released in 1981 after making just 18 league appearances in two seasons with the club. Cohen dies aged just 54 in 2010 following a motorcycle accident.

SATURDAY 15th NOVEMBER 1969

Match of the Day goes colour for the first time and, just as the first black and white edition was, the cameras broadcast from Anfield as Liverpool take on West Ham United. Chris Lawler and Bobby Graham score a goal in each half in the 2-0 victory over the Hammers.

SATURDAY 15th NOVEMBER 2008

Liverpool make the short trip to Bolton, and return to Anfield with all three points, thanks to a 2-0 win at the Reebok Stadium. Consistent Dutchman Dirk Kuyt gets the Reds' first goal in the 28th minute. Typically, captain Steven Gerrard gets himself on the score-sheet when it matters, as he nets Liverpool's second with just over 15 minutes to play to put Rafa Benitez's side level on points at the top with Chelsea, and eight clear of Manchester United.

SATURDAY 16th NOVEMBER 1985

Liverpool defeat West Bromwich Albion at Anfield in their First Division clash. It would take until the final moments of the first half for the home side to get into the game as Steve Nicol equalises after Albion had taken the lead in the 38th minute. The second period was all Liverpool's as Jan Molby, Mark Lawrenson and Paul Walsh all grab a goal each to give the Reds a 4-1 win.

WEDNESDAY 16th NOVEMBER 1994

Neil Ruddock earns his one cap having been called up by Terry Venables for a friendly match against Nigeria. The defender has previously played for both England under-21s and the B side. This was to be his only appearances for his country at full international level. England win 1-0 at Wembley thanks to a goal from captain David Platt.

SATURDAY 17th NOVEMBER 1934

Gordon Hodgson hits a hat-trick as Liverpool defeat Leicester City 5-1 at Anfield. The South African striker scores Liverpool's first three – netting all of his goals before the hour mark – including two within 60 seconds. In the final ten minutes both Vic Wright and Harold Taylor net one each to complete the scoring.

TUESDAY 17th NOVEMBER 1959

After a shaky start to the season, Phil Taylor resigns as Liverpool manager after being unable to lead the club back to Division One. Taylor left on a losing note as his side crumbled to a 4-2 defeat against Lincoln City at Sincil Bank. The former Liverpool defender, who joined the club as an inside-forward when signed from Bristol Rovers by George Patterson, believes that the strain of trying to gain promotion was what led to him stepping down as manager.

SATURDAY 18th NOVEMBER 1972

Liverpool defeat Newcastle United 3-2 at Anfield in front of 46,513 in a First Division match. Peter Cormack, Alec Lindsay and John Toshack are the men on target for the home side. Even Tommy Smith's missed penalty in the 68th minute is not significant as Liverpool take the points on the day.

MARK LAWRENSON — PART OF THE DREAM BACK FOUR THAT INCLUDED KENNEDY, NEAL AND HANSEN (SEE 16TH NOVEMBER 1985).

TUESDAY 18th NOVEMBER 1997

Michael Owen proves his potential as a footballer by netting a hat-trick in a League Cup fourth-round tie against Grimsby Town. The young striker shows his talent by netting three times in a half hour period either side of half-time, which confirms Liverpool's progression as they earn a 3-1 win over the Mariners.

SATURDAY 19th NOVEMBER 1988

Liverpool's First Division clash with Queens Park Rangers at Loftus Road ends in a 1-0 victory for the visitors. John Aldridge is the hero, scoring the only goal of the match in the 28th minute to ensure the points go back to the north-west. The striker is substituted with 18 minutes left on the clock as Steve Staunton is brought on to make sure Liverpool maintain their lead.

SATURDAY 19th NOVEMBER 2005

Despite a missed penalty from Peter Crouch, Liverpool manage to win 3-0 against Portsmouth at Anfield. Crouch's spot kick is saved but Bolo Zenden follows up to head home the opener from the rebound. The other goals come from Djibril Cisse and Fernando Morientes as Liverpool earn the three points.

SATURDAY 20th NOVEMBER 1954

One of Liverpool's many South Africans during the 1950s, Doug Rudham makes his debut for the club in a Second Division match against Nottingham Forest at home. The goalkeeper manages to keep a clean sheet as Billy Liddell's 49th-minute penalty was the only difference between the two teams. Rudham never successfully cements his place in goal, making 66 appearances in five years at Anfield.

SATURDAY 20th NOVEMBER 2010

A lowly West Ham United are despatched at Anfield as Liverpool stroll to a 3-0 victory. Former Hammer Glen Johnson opens the scoring in the 18th minute as he slams home from 18 yards following a Raul Meireles corner. Dirk Kuyt calmly slots a penalty past Rob Green nine minutes later, and Maxi Rodriguez rounds off the scoring before the interval to confirm three welcome points.

SATURDAY 21st NOVEMBER 1896

Alf Milward becomes the first-ever player to be sent off in a Merseyside derby when the Everton man is dismissed in the game at Anfield. The Toffees player was removed from the field following a 'charge' on John McCartney. Despite being down to ten men, the visitors manage to hold on for a goalless draw.

SATURDAY 21st NOVEMBER 1998

It takes a Robbie Fowler hat-trick for Liverpool to overcome Aston Villa in Birmingham. Paul Ince scores in the second minute to give the visitors an early lead, with Fowler adding another five minutes later. The striker completes his triple in the second period by netting twice within ten minutes as Liverpool win 4-2.

SATURDAY 22nd NOVEMBER 1952

Local boy Ronnie Moran makes his debut for the club in a 3-2 loss at Derby County. The 18-year-old defender goes on to make 343 league appearances over a 16-year period at Anfield, winning both the Second and First Division titles whilst playing for Liverpool. After retirement he would stay on the Liverpool coaching staff for almost 30 years, including two stints as caretaker manager.

WEDNESDAY 22nd NOVEMBER 2006

PSV Eindhoven are seen off 2-0 at Anfield in the Champions League group phase. Liverpool's game starts badly as Mark Gonzalez and Xabi Alonso are both injured in the first half. The Reds come into their own in the second period as Steven Gerrard and Peter Crouch both hit the back of the net to give Liverpool the points.

TUESDAY 23rd NOVEMBER 2004

Javier Saviola's handball goes unpunished in the lead-up to Monaco's only goal as Liverpool lose 1-0 at the Stade Louis II. Danish referee Claus Bo Larsen saw himself at the centre of the controversy as he missed the illegal action from the Argentine striker. Rafa Benitez would later claim that all the officials admitted to seeing the handball, but failed to act appropriately.

TUESDAY 24th NOVEMBER 1987

Liverpool despatch Watford at Anfield 4-0 in front of 32,296 spectators. There are four different scorers for the Reds as Steve McMahon nets the first in the 54th minute, before Ray Houghton, John Aldridge and John Barnes complete the scoring with all the goals coming in a quarter-of-an-hour spell in the second period.

SATURDAY 24th NOVEMBER 2007

Liverpool travel to St James' Park, running out 3-0 winners against Newcastle United in front of 53,307. Steven Gerrard netted the first by slamming a free kick home in the 27th minute. Dirk Kuyt saw the ball bounce in off his shin to double the lead, before his fellow Dutchman Ryan Babel came off the bench to net the third.

WEDNESDAY 25th NOVEMBER 1964

An entirely red kit is worn for the first time by Liverpool as the team take on Anderlecht in a European Cup tie at Anfield. It is believed that Bill Shankly made the decision to change the team's attire as he thought that the completely red outfit would make his side look more powerful. It works on its first outing as Liverpool beat the Belgians 3-0, thanks to goals from Ian St John, Roger Hunt and Ron Yeats. Since that day the club's official home kit has remained the same.

SATURDAY 25th NOVEMBER 2006

Liverpool beat Manchester City 1-0 in the Premier League. The game is a struggle for the Reds as City pack the midfield to try and thwart Liverpool in the centre of the park with the only goal coming from Steven Gerrard in the 66th minute.

WEDNESDAY 26th NOVEMBER 1969

Liverpool defeat Portuguese side Vitoria Setúbal at Anfield in a European Cup second-round clash. A difficult task is made worse, as the visitors took a two-goal lead. However, Tommy Smith, Alun Evans and Roger Hunt score to give Liverpool the win on the night, but it just wasn't enough to see the team progress. Despite the win, the Reds were still knocked out of the competition having lost the away leg 1-0.

WEDNESDAY 26th NOVEMBER 2008

Steven Gerrard nets the only goal as Liverpool beat Marseille at Anfield in a Champions League group game. The midfielder had a quiet game, but his header from a Xabi Alonso cross in the 23rd minute sees Liverpool record the victory at Anfield in front of over 40,000 fans, who witnessed the Reds earn the three points.

TUESDAY 27th NOVEMBER 1990

Don Hutchison signs from Hartlepool United. The youngster enjoys a brief spell in the first team at Victoria Park having come through the club's youth system. Manager Kenny Dalglish buys Hutchison, as he looks to the club's future. It would be 18 months before the midfielder makes his debut for Liverpool. He stays at the club for four years, before being sold to West Ham United.

WEDNESDAY 27th NOVEMBER 1996

Robbie Fowler scores twice as Liverpool overcome Arsenal in a League Cup fourth-round tie at Anfield. The striker nets either side of half-time, as his goals are sandwiched between strikes from Steve McManaman and Czech winger Patrick Berger to see Liverpool through to the next round of the competition.

SUNDAY 28th NOVEMBER 1993

Liverpool beat Aston Villa 2-1 at Anfield, thanks to goals from Robbie Fowler and Jamie Redknapp. The young striker is just starting his career with the club, having made his debut two months previously. Fowler scored with almost the final touch of the first period, with Redknapp netting the winner just after the hour mark.

WEDNESDAY 28th NOVEMBER 2007

A double from Spanish striker Fernando Torres sets Liverpool on their way to a 4-1 win over Porto at Anfield in the Champions League Group A clash. The Portuguese side were no match for the Reds, with the home team taking a 2-1 lead into the final 12 minutes thanks to strikes from Torres, before Steven Gerrard and Peter Crouch score the goals that guarantee victory that keeps the dream of reaching the knockout round alive.

WEDNESDAY 29th NOVEMBER 2000

Liverpool hit eight goals to defeat Stoke City in the League Cup at the Britannia Stadium. Robbie Fowler gets three of the Reds' goals, with the other strikes coming from five different scorers, as Christian Ziege, Vladimir Smicer, Markus Babbel, Sami Hyypia and Danny Murphy all get their names on the score-sheet.

THURSDAY 29th NOVEMBER 2001

Club legend Robbie Fowler is sold to Leeds United for a fee of £11m. Fowler came up through the club's ranks, making his first-team debut in 1993 and going on to score 183 goals in 369 appearances for Liverpool. Following spells at Elland Road, and later, Manchester City, the striker would return to Anfield for an 18-month stint from January 2006, before being released.

WEDNESDAY 30th NOVEMBER 1994

Ian Rush scores a hat-trick at Ewood Park to give Liverpool a 3-1 win over Blackburn Rovers in the League Cup. It's a great result for the Reds, considering that Rovers will go on to win the Premier League title at the end of the season. The Welsh striker scored the opener after 19 minutes as he struck a left-footed shot into the top corner from the edge of the area. In the 57th minute he would get the better of Tim Flowers in a one-on-one to double the advantage, before toe-poking home a cross with 20 minutes to go in order to guarantee Liverpool's progression.

WEDNESDAY 30th NOVEMBER 2005

Liverpool see off Sunderland 2-0 at the Stadium of Light in their Premier League clash. The damage was done in the first half as Luis Garcia and Steven Gerrard score to give the Reds an unassailable lead. The only downside to the win is the dismissal of Mohamed Sissoko who is sent off for two bookable offences.

SATURDAY 30th NOVEMBER 2005

Steve McManaman scores the only goal of the game as Liverpool beat Arsenal 1-0 at Highbury. It's the Gunners' first home loss since May and the victory lifts the Reds to seventh in the Premier League.

LIVERPOOL FC
On This Day

DECEMBER

SATURDAY 1st DECEMBER 1974

Peter Cormack's goal on 14 minutes is enough to preserve Liverpool's 100% home record with a 1-0 victory over West Ham United. It's the Reds' ninth consecutive home victory – a contrast with the form on the road which had seen Liverpool win just one of their nine games – the main reason leaders Leeds United are six points clear at the top.

SATURDAY 1st DECEMBER 1979

Liverpool stay on the shoulders of league leaders Manchester United with a thumping 4-0 victory over Middlesbrough at Anfield. It's the fifth time in the first 17 games that the Reds have hit four goals and the scorers on this occasion are Terry McDermott, Alan Hansen, David Johnson and Ray Kennedy.

SATURDAY 1st DECEMBER 1984

Jan Molby scores his first goal for Liverpool in a 3-1 defeat to Chelsea at Stamford Bridge. It would be the first of 61 goals from the Danish midfielder in a Liverpool career that spanned nearly 12 years. The former Ajax midfielder, who won 33 caps for his country, scored on his last appearance for Liverpool in a 3-2 defeat against Coventry City at Anfield.

MONDAY 1st DECEMBER 1997

Haukur Ingi Gudnason signs for £150,000 but the Icelandic forward fails to make the grade at Anfield. Gudnason makes it to the Liverpool bench on three occasions but is never called upon and after suffering several injuries, he returns to Iceland after three frustrating years on Merseyside.

SATURDAY 2nd DECEMBER 1978

Liverpool lose only their second game of the season after Arsenal win 1-0 at Highbury. Almost 52,000 fans watch the match and the majority go home happy with the result. The Reds will only lose twice more all season on their way to the title. Everton and Bristol City both beat Bob Paisley's side 1-0 and Aston Villa dish out the heaviest loss of the 1978/79 campaign, winning 3-1 at Villa Park. Only two points are dropped at Anfield all season – quite a record.

SATURDAY 2nd DECEMBER 1989

Nick Tanner makes his Liverpool debut in a 4-1 win over Manchester City at Maine Road. The central defender comes on after 16 minutes for the injured Gary Gillespie some 16 months after signing from Bristol Rovers for £20,000. Tanner would go on to make 59 appearances for the Reds, spending almost five years at Anfield as mostly an understudy for the more experienced defenders ahead of him. He also spent time on loan with Norwich City and Swindon Town before leaving Merseyside after persistent back problems. He was forced to retire from the game in 1994, aged 29.

SUNDAY 2nd DECEMBER 2007

A crowd of 43,270 watches Liverpool beat Bolton Wanderers 4-0 at Anfield, with goals from Sami Hyypia, Fernando Torres, a Steven Gerrard penalty and a Ryan Babel strike in the last five minutes. The club were free scoring at the time having beat Besiktas 8-0 and Porto 4-1 at Anfield in the Champions League, either side of a 2-0 victory at home to Fulham, and a 3-0 victory against Newcastle United at St James' Park.

SATURDAY 3rd DECEMBER 1892

John Miller becomes the first Liverpool player to score five goals in a match, while Matt McQueen scores his first-ever goal for the club as Fleetwood Rangers are thrashed 7-0 at Anfield in the Lancashire League. McQueen gave Liverpool the lead and Malcolm McVean added a second before Miller stole the show with a five-goal haul to compound Fleetwood's misery to the delight of the home crowd.

TUESDAY 3rd DECEMBER 1968

Ian Callaghan's goal on 14 minutes gives Liverpool a hard-fought 1-0 win over Southampton at Anfield. The midweek victory keeps the Reds four points clear of nearest challengers Everton and Leeds United in joint second.

SATURDAY 3rd DECEMBER 1977

Goals from Kenny Dalglish and David Fairclough give Liverpool a 2-0 victory over West Ham United at Anfield. It is Dalglish's ninth league goal of the season and keeps the Reds in fourth place, four points behind leaders Nottingham Forest.

SATURDAY 3rd DECEMBER 1983

Liverpool make hard work of beating lowly Birmingham City at Anfield. Ian Rush spares the Reds' blushes with a goal on 86 minutes to maintain top spot, although just 24,791 fans are there to see it.

SATURDAY 3rd DECEMBER 2005

Peter Crouch finally scores a goal for Liverpool and, like buses, when he'd scored one another came along straight after. The beanpole striker joined Liverpool in July 2005 from Southampton for £7m, but many wondered if it had been a waste of money as Crouch went game after game without finding the back of the net. Rafa Benitez kept faith in his signing but even his patience must have been wearing thin after his 18th game without a goal. Finally, against Wigan Athletic, Crouch ended his drought after 1,229 minutes without a goal. Crouch remained at Anfield for three years before joining Portsmouth and left with a respectable record of 42 goals in 134 appearances.

SATURDAY 4th DECEMBER 1909

Liverpool complete one of the greatest comebacks in the club's history as they come from 5-2 down at half-time to beat Newcastle United 6-5 at Anfield. Former Glossop winger Arthur Goddard got his name on the score-sheet, as did former Motherwell winger James Stewart. Ronald Orr, who also played for Glossop, and Jack Parkinson scored twice to complete a remarkable turnaround on a frosty December afternoon.

SATURDAY 4th DECEMBER 1971

Liverpool earn a decent point after drawing 0-0 away to Ipswich Town, but it comes during one of the most barren months in front of goal in the Reds' recent history. Despite beating Derby County 3-2 in the next game, Liverpool then fail to score in the next five games meaning they'd fired blanks in six out of seven games. No doubt John Toshack's absence through injury is one of the main reasons behind the Reds' drought. His return sparks a 4-1 win at home to Crystal Palace and the victories and goals begin to flow again with Shankly's men winning 13 out of 14 games, scoring 34 goals and conceding just three!

PETER CROUCH GETS OFF THE MARK AT ANFIELD (SEE 3RD DECEMBER 2005).

SATURDAY 5th DECEMBER 1970

John Toshack scores his second Anfield goal in a 1-1 draw with Leeds United – his second in his first four games for the club. The big Welsh striker was brought to Anfield from Cardiff City in 1970 for a fee of £110,000 but soon convinced the Liverpool fans he was worth the money. Superb in the air, when Kevin Keegan joined in 1971 the pair struck up an understanding often described as 'telepathic' with Toshack often winning aerial duels and Keegan profiting from his knock-downs. He remained on Merseyside for eight years, scoring 96 goals in 246 appearances.

SUNDAY 5th DECEMBER 1999

Steven Gerrard scores his first goal for Liverpool, the third in a 4-1 victory over Sheffield Wednesday at Anfield. Having made his debut as a substitute for Vegard Heggem in a 2-0 win at home to Blackburn Rovers, the academy graduate finally got his first goal for the club, adding to those of Sami Hyypia and Danny Murphy, before David Thompson added a fourth to round off an impressive victory for Gerard Houllier's team.

SATURDAY 6th DECEMBER 1902

Sam Raybould scores four goals as Liverpool comprehensively beat Grimsby Town 9-2 in a Division One clash at Anfield. Edgar Chadwick and Arthur Goddard both scored twice, while George Livingstone completed the scoring. The result put the club on course for a fifth-place finish in the league, while the Mariners succumbed to relegation at the end of the campaign, along with Bolton Wanderers.

TUESDAY 6th DECEMBER 1994

Ian Rush scores the fifth goal in a 6-0 thrashing of Celtic in his testimonial at Anfield to celebrate his 14th season as a Liverpool player. The Welshman was joined on the score-sheet by Phil Babb, Stig Inge Bjornebye, Steve McManaman, Neil Ruddock and the unfortunate Mark McNally, who put the ball into his own goal. Rush continued to play for Liverpool until 1995, when he left to join Leeds United after scoring 336 goals in 660 appearances. He remains the club's all-time greatest goal scorer and is unlikely to be beaten anytime soon.

WEDNESDAY 7th DECEMBER 1966

Ajax beat Liverpool 5-1 in the European Cup second round, first leg at the Olympisch Stadion in Amsterdam. Cornelis de Wolf got the Dutch champions off to the perfect start when he beat Tommy Lawler inside the opening three minutes. Johan Cruyff made it 2-0, before Klaas Nuninga netted two more before half-time. Hendrik Groot added a fifth before Chris Lawler scored a mere consolation for Bill Shankly's team.

WEDNESDAY 8th DECEMBER 2004

Rafael Benitez makes three game-changing substitutions as Liverpool beat Olympiacos 3-1 to seal their passage into the knockout phase of the Champions League. Trailing 1-0 at half-time thanks to a goal from World Cup winner Rivaldo, Benitez introduces Florent Sinama-Pongolle in place of Djimi Traore, and within minutes of his arrival, the Frenchman had equalised. With Liverpool needing to score twice to progress, Benitez threw caution to the wind and brought on Neil Mellor and Josemi. Mellor scored two minutes after replacing Milan Baros before Steven Gerrard crashed home the decisive goal just seconds after Josemi's introduction to send Liverpool through.

SATURDAY 9th DECEMBER 1905

Sam Raybould scores his 100th goal for Liverpool in only his 162nd appearance for the club, as Liverpool beat Wolverhampton Wanderers 4-0 at Anfield. The striker, who was never capped for England despite his prolific goalscoring record for Liverpool, netted his first goal in only his second game for the club, a 3-1 defeat against local rivals Everton at Goodison Park. Raybould went on to score a further 30 goals in 64 games before joining Sunderland at the age of 32.

SATURDAY 9th DECEMBER 1967

Roger Hunt, and a comical Gary Sprake own goal, give Liverpool a 2-0 win over Leeds United at Anfield. Both goals come in the first half.

WEDNESDAY 9th DECEMBER 2008

Jay Spearing makes his debut in a 3-1 win away to PSV Eindhoven. The Wirral-born academy graduate comes on after 76 minutes for Albert Riera. Martin Kelly also makes his debut and David N'Gog scores his first Liverpool goal on a satisfying evening for Rafa Benitez.

SATURDAY 10th DECEMBER 1983

Joe Fagan watches his Division One pacesetting side capitulate in a shocking 90 minutes at Highfield Road as Coventry City romp home 4-0. The Reds were 3-0 down at half-time and conceded another after the break. As a result, Manchester United and West Ham United move to within one point of Liverpool and Coventry City move up to fourth. Fagan demands a response in the next game and gets it, with poor Notts County on the receiving end of a 5-0 thrashing at Anfield. The Reds bide their time for revenge against the Sky Blues and return the compliment handed out in the East Midlands by beating City 5-0 in the return fixture later in the campaign.

TUESDAY 10th DECEMBER 1985

Charlie Adam is born in Dundee. The cultured midfielder has an unusual path to Anfield via Rangers, Ross County, St Mirren and finally Blackpool, from whom he signs for the Reds at a cost of £8.5m. Though Adam enjoyed mixed fortunes at Ibrox, it was when he was bought by Blackpool boss Ian Holloway that he really came to the fore as a player. Adam was the heart and soul of the Seasiders' successful drive for promotion to the Premier League and was one of the players of the year during Blackpool's season among the elite. Liverpool tried to sign him before the January 2011 transfer window closed but Holloway described the offer as 'derisory'. Following relegation Kenny Dalglish returned for the Scot and by July 7th, he was a Liverpool player.

SUNDAY 10th DECEMBER 2000

Igor Biscan makes his Liverpool debut in a 1-0 defeat at home to newly-promoted, and high-flying, Ipswich Town. Marcus Stewart scores the only goal as the Tractor Boys continued their surprising form en route to a Uefa Cup place. Biscan joined the club from Dinamo Zagreb and spent five seasons at Anfield before becoming a victim of the 'Rafalution'. When his contract expired in July 2005, he returned to his native Croatia, re-joining Zagreb.

SATURDAY 11th DECEMBER 1937

Fewer than 16,000 see Bolton Wanderers hold Liverpool to a 0-0 draw at Burnden Park. It's only a third clean sheet for a leaky Reds defence.

CHARLIE ADAM – PROTRACTED TRANSFER TO THE REDS BUT A WELCOME ADDITION TO KENNY DALGLISH'S SIDE (SEE 10TH DECEMBER 1985).

SATURDAY 11th DECEMBER 1954

Liverpool suffer their biggest-ever defeat at the hands of Birmingham City in a 9-1 defeat at St Andrew's. Billy Liddell scored the only goal for the visitors, who fell 3-0 down inside the opening 15 minutes of the game. Striker Alan A'Court believes that the pitch was largely to blame for Liverpool's downfall, saying that the players kept slipping and sliding, but admitted that Birmingham suffered the same problems too.

SATURDAY 11th DECEMBER 1994

Liverpool remain in fourth place after a 0-0 draw with Crystal Palace at Anfield.

TUESDAY 11th DECEMBER 2000

Erik Meijer leaves Liverpool after 17 months. The journeyman striker joined on a free transfer from Bayer Leverkusen but fails to really make an impact during his time at Anfield. Despite this, he proves to be a popular figure among Reds fans and though he only plays 27 times and scores two goals, his stay is largely enjoyable.

WEDNESDAY 11th DECEMBER 2007

Liverpool travel to Marseille knowing failure to win will mean an exit from the Champions League. Within four minutes, however, the Reds are ahead through Steven Gerrard and Fernando Torres adds a second soon after. With the majority of the 53,000 crowd silenced, Dirk Kuyt and Ryan Babel add further goals to give the Reds a stunning 4-0 victory and a passage into the knockout rounds. Gerrard's goal also makes him Liverpool's record goal scorer in European competition.

WEDNESDAY 12th DECEMBER 1984

Daniel Agger is born in Hvidovre, Denmark. He began his career at Rosenhoj as a youth player before joining Brondby IF at the age of 12, where he went on to make 49 appearances and earn an international call-up before becoming the most expensive Danish player to be sold to a foreign club when he signed for Liverpool in a £6m deal on January 12th 2006. He made his debut on February 1st in a 1-1 draw with Birmingham City at Anfield.

TUESDAY 13th DECEMBER 2005

Lethal striker Fernando Morientes joins Liverpool in a deal believed to be in the region of £8m from Spanish giants Real Madrid. The former Albacete striker had been on loan at Monaco the previous season and impressed during the club's Champions League campaign, where he scored crucial goals against Real Madrid and Chelsea en route to the final, but was helpless as Porto won the competition following a 3-0 win. But, the Spaniard had a dip in form when he arrived in Merseyside and only managed nine goals in his two seasons with the club, and was eventually sold to Valencia for £3m.

WEDNESDAY 13th DECEMBER 2000

For the first time in Liverpool's history, two subs score in a domestic game as the Reds beat Fulham 3-0 in the League Cup. The Cottagers put up a brave battle and force the game into extra time but bench-warmers for the night Michael Owen and Nick Barmby – plus another from Vladimir Smicer – see the Reds home with three goals in the last 15 minutes.

FRIDAY 14th DECEMBER 1979

Michael Owen is born in Chester, England. No-one would have guessed that Michael James Owen would grow up to be one of the most feared strikers in world football after he burst onto the Premier League scene in 1997, scoring on his debut after coming on as a substitute for Patrick Berger during a 2-1 defeat against Wimbledon at Selhurst Park. Owen went on to score 158 goals in 297 appearances for Liverpool before joining Real Madrid in an £8m deal in 2004. He won an FA Cup, a Uefa Cup and two League Cups during his time at Anfield.

SATURDAY 15th DECEMBER 1990

Steve McManaman makes his Liverpool debut, coming off the bench for Peter Beardsley in a 2-0 win over Sheffield United at Anfield. John Barnes and Ian Rush had scored the goals before 'Macca' made the first of 364 appearances for the club. His first of 66 goals came in a 2-1 defeat to Manchester City at Maine Road on August 21st 1991. McManaman scored his last goal – the winner – in a 3-2 victory over Tottenham Hotspur at Anfield on May 1st 1999 before joining Real Madrid for £6m.

MONDAY 16th DECEMBER 1991

Two years after scoring the championship-winning goal for Arsenal at Anfield, England international Michael Thomas completes his transfer from the Gunners in a £1.5m deal. Thomas made his debut in a 2-1 victory over Spurs at White Hart Lane and scored the first goal in the club's FA Cup triumph over Sunderland in 1992, when he converted Steve McManaman's cross. Thomas joined Portuguese side Benfica, managed then by former Liverpool manager Graeme Souness, in 1998.

SATURDAY 17th DECEMBER 1955

Jimmy Melia scores a debut goal as Liverpool beat Nottingham Forest 5-2 at Anfield. The playmaker, who joined Liverpool at the age of 15, broke onto the scene as a 19-year-old and went on to make 286 appearances for the club, scoring 79 goals. He finished as Liverpool's top goalscorer in the 1958/59 campaign, with 21 in 40 games as Liverpool finished fourth in the Second Division. He joined Wolverhampton Wanderers in 1964, before ending his career as player-coach at Crewe Alexandra, where he took up the managerial position full-time.

WEDNESDAY 18th DECEMBER 2002

Danny Murphy scores a last-gasp winner as Liverpool beat Aston Villa 4-3 in a League Cup fifth-round tie at Villa Park. Darius Vassell opened the scoring when he converted a penalty midway through the first half, before Murphy brought the scores level. Milan Baros and Steven Gerrard appeared to put the game to bed with second-half goals, but Thomas Hitzlsperger and a Stefan Henchoz own goal made it 3-3, before Murphy netted his second of the game to see Liverpool safely through to the semi-finals of the competition they went on to win.

SATURDAY 19th DECEMBER 1997

Liverpool complete the signing of goalkeeper Brad Friedel from Columbus Crew in a £1.7m deal. Both Nottingham Forest and Newcastle United had attempted to sign him a few seasons before his move to Anfield, but neither club could secure a work permit. The American was also attracting interest from both Celtic and Rangers, but opted for a move to the Premier League. He spent three seasons at Anfield, mainly behind David James and then Sander Westerveld, before signing for Blackburn Rovers in 2000.

SATURDAY 20th DECEMBER 1975

Liverpool replace QPR at the top of Division One following a terrific 2-0 win at Anfield. The title race hots up with just three points separating seven clubs in the battle for the title. John Toshack puts the Reds ahead on 22 minutes and Phil Neal seals the points from the penalty spot on 75 minutes to send the near-40,000 crowd home happy. The victory is sweet revenge for the 2-0 opening-day defeat at Loftus Road.

SATURDAY 20th DECEMBER 1986

Liverpool lose ground on the leaders after failing to beat third-bottom Charlton Athletic at The Valley. The 0-0 draw allows Everton to move onto the same points as the Reds, with a 3-0 win over Wimbledon.

THURSDAY 20th DECEMBER 2001

France international Nicolas Anelka joins Liverpool on loan from Paris St Germain for the remainder of the campaign. The former Arsenal and Real Madrid striker scored four times in the league and once in the FA Cup as Liverpool finished second in the Premier League. But manager Gerard Houllier decided against making the loan a permanent deal, and opted to sign Senegal striker El-Hadji Diouf from Lens after he impressed at the 2002 World Cup in South Korea and Japan. Anelka moved to Manchester City for £13m at the start of the next campaign.

SATURDAY 21st DECEMBER 1957

Tony McNamara scores on his debut as Liverpool beat Bristol City at Anfield in a Second Division game. The Liverpool-born winger started his career at Everton, and made the short move across Stanley Park after making 111 appearances for the Toffees. However, McNamara only made ten appearances for Liverpool and chose to join Division Four outfit Crewe Alexandra at the end of the campaign, stepping down three divisions in total having played for Everton in Division One.

SATURDAY 21st DECEMBER 1991

Liverpool come from behind to earn a point against Manchester City at Anfield. Dean Saunders, a boyhood City fan, puts the Reds ahead in the first half but the Blues come back strongly with two David White goals but are denied a first win away to Liverpool for a decade by Steve Nicol's 83rd-minute equaliser.

THURSDAY 22nd DECEMBER 1983

Liverpool play the quickest replay in the club's history after drawing 1-1 with Birmingham City at St Andrew's in the League Cup fourth round. The Reds play Blues just two days after the draw but less than 12,000 can be bothered attending the match at Anfield as Joe Fagan's side comprehensively win 3-0 courtesy of a goal from Steve Nicol, and a brace from Ian Rush. Liverpool go on to win the trophy after a final replay against Everton is settled by Graeme Souness' 21st-minute goal in front of a 52,009 crowd at Manchester City's Maine Road.

SATURDAY 22nd DECEMBER 2002

Liverpool stay behind Everton in the Premier League after a disappointing 0-0 draw at Anfield. With the Toffees in fourth place, the chance to overtake was lost and the Reds slipped yet further behind leaders Arsenal. The game's only memorable moment is Steve Gerrard's rash tackle on Gary Naysmith for which the Liverpool captain is lucky not to be shown a straight red card by referee Graham Poll.

SATURDAY 22nd DECEMBER 2007

Fernando Torres scores twice as Liverpool beat Portsmouth 4-1 in a Premier League fixture at Anfield. Israeli Yossi Benayoun gave Rafael Benitez's team the lead after 13 minutes, before a Sylvain Distin own goal three minutes later doubled Liverpool's advantage. Benjani pulled a goal back just before the hour mark before Torres put the game beyond doubt with two well-taken goals. The Spaniard was then replaced by Lucas as Benitez looked to shore up his defence.

SATURDAY 23rd DECEMBER 1972

John Toshack scores two first-half goals as Liverpool ease past Coventry City at Anfield. The 2-0 victory keeps the Reds two points clear at the top and maintains Bill Shankly's team's 100% home record having won all 11 home fixtures so far.

SATURDAY 23rd DECEMBER 1989

Manchester United earn a 0-0 draw at Anfield to deny Liverpool top spot in Division One. The Reds go into the game in second spot but can't break down a resolute United rearguard and have to settle for a point.

FERNANDO TORRES – ONE OF THE MOST EXCITING STRIKERS SEEN AT ANFIELD FOR MANY YEARS (SEE 22ND DECEMBER 2007).

SATURDAY 23rd DECEMBER 2000

Three second-half goals from Michael Owen, Nicky Barmby and Robbie Fowler round off a terrific display as Arsenal are brushed aside with consummate ease at Anfield. Steven Gerrard put Liverpool ahead with a little over ten minutes played before the three goals after the hour mark completed a 4-0 victory over the Gunners, who would go on to win the Premier League.

SATURDAY 24th DECEMBER 1938

Jack Balmer's second-half goal is little consolation as Liverpool are beaten 4-1 at Chelsea. The Pensioners climb from second-bottom as a result of the win, while the Reds' hopes of promotion take a severe blow they never quite recover from, eventually finishing 11th.

SATURDAY 24th DECEMBER 1949

Willie Fagan scores Liverpool's 3,000th goal as he nets the second in a 3-1 win over local rivals Everton in front of 50,485 spectators at Anfield. Kevin Barron scored the 2,999th and then scored the 3,001st to complete the scoring and continue the club's fine goalscoring form. The manager at the time was George Kay.

SATURDAY 24th DECEMBER 1966

An Alan Hinton own goal, and a strike from Geoff Strong on 39 minutes, gives Liverpool a 2-0 half-time lead at Chelsea on Christmas Eve. Though the Blues pull one back after the break, the 2-1 victory means the Reds climb above Chelsea into second spot in Division One. The result means Chelsea have won just three of a dozen home games, while remaining unbeaten in all ten away matches!

SATURDAY 25th DECEMBER 1954

Billy Liddell enjoys a terrific Christmas as he scores four goals in Liverpool's 6-2 victory over Ipswich Town at Anfield. The victory is the perfect riposte to two heavy league defeats in the previous two games to Birmingham City and Doncaster Rovers during which 13 goals were conceded. Though Liverpool's home form is that of a team destined for promotion, the team they defeat are rooted to the foot of Division Two and when the two teams meet again the following day (as was the way back then) Ipswich win 2-0.

WEDNESDAY 25th DECEMBER 1957

Division Two leaders Liverpool suffer a shock 3-1 defeat at Grimsby Town on Christmas Day. The defeat highlights the Reds' poor form on the road just as the 3-2 victory over the same opponents a day later at Anfield shows Liverpool's strength on home soil.

FRIDAY 25th DECEMBER 1964

Gary McAllister is born in Motherwell, Scotland. The midfielder joined Liverpool on a free transfer from Coventry City at the age of 35 and went on to make 87 appearances in two seasons. He was heavily involved in the club's thrilling Uefa Cup Final victory over Alaves in Dortmund, where he was involved in four of Liverpool's five goals in the 5-4 win. McAllister re-joined Coventry in 2002 as player-manager.

WEDNESDAY 26th DECEMBER 1928

Liverpool feast on goals and Claret as Burnley are crushed at Anfield on a wonderful Boxing Day outing for Matt McQueen's team. Bill Salisbury got his name on the score-sheet for the hosts, while James Clark and Dick Edmed both scored twice. But it was Gordon Hodgson who stole the headlines with a sensational hat-trick as Liverpool strolled to an 8-0 victory, with the Clarets clearly feeling the effects of the festive period. It could have been better for the Reds, but Robert Done missed a penalty.

WEDNESDAY 26th DECEMBER 1958

Brisbane Road is silenced by Phil Taylor's Liverpool side who ran out 4-0 winners against Leyton Orient in a Division Two clash. The Reds registered four different scorers on a frosty afternoon in the capital. Alan A'Court, Alan Arnell, Billy Liddell and Louis Bimpson all hit the back of the net as Liverpool continue their push for a return back to England's top flight. Unfortunately, the club could only finish third, missing out on promotion by one point.

TUESDAY 26th DECEMBER 1961

Leaders Liverpool are surprisingly beaten 1-0 at Millmoor. It is a second successive blow following a 1-0 defeat to Leeds United just three days earlier. The Reds maintain a four-point lead over nearest challengers Leyton Orient.

THURSDAY 26th DECEMBER 1963

Roger Hunt hits a fantastic four goals as Liverpool cruise to victory over Stoke City in a fabulous feast of festive football at Anfield. The striker, who was part of England's 1966 World Cup-winning side, got all of his goals in the second half at Anfield, adding to Ian St John's ninth-minute opener, while Alf Arrowsmith got the other for Liverpool, who treated the home fans to a very merry Christmas.

THURSDAY 26th DECEMBER 1968

Chris Lawler scores Liverpool's equaliser in a disappointing 1-1 draw with Burnley at Anfield. Nicknamed 'the ghost', Lawler was an elegant right-back who supported the attack with great aplomb and had a knack of scoring vital goals, too, notching 61 in 546 league games. Another Shankly favourite, Lawler was dependable and economic in possession.

FRIDAY 26th DECEMBER 1969

Peter Thompson is among the scorers as Liverpool serve up a festive treat beating Burnley 5-1 at Turf Moor. Thompson was a cultured winger who Bill Shankly played throughout his Anfield tenure. Even Everton legend Dixie Dean admitted he would have loved to have played alongside Thompson. Ian Callaghan said that if he had, he would have scored even more than the 60 league goals he managed in one incredible season. Technically brilliant, skilful and a terrific crosser, Thompson was a first-team regular for more than a decade, making 416 appearances in total.

TUESDAY 26th DECEMBER 1978

Liverpool's Christmas gets even better with a 3-0 victory over fierce rivals Manchester United at Old Trafford. Ray Kennedy got Bob Paisley's team off to the perfect start, as he netted the opener after five minutes to silence the home crowd. Just 20 minutes later, Jimmy Case doubled the Reds' lead before David Fairclough ended the goalscoring midway through the second half. It was only the second meeting between the two sides on Boxing Day, and they went on to play each other on the same day for the next two seasons, the Reds winning one 2-0 and drawing the other 0-0. A year later, Liverpool beat Manchester City 3-1.

FRIDAY 26th DECEMBER 1997

Second-half goals from Michael Owen and two from Robbie Fowler seal a comfortable 3-1 victory over high-flying Leeds United at Anfield. Owen gave Liverpool the lead just one minute after the restart, and fellow academy graduate Fowler added a second on 79 minutes. Just four minutes later, Fowler put the game beyond doubt before Alfie Haaland added a late consolation goal for the Elland Road side.

SUNDAY 26th DECEMBER 2004

Liverpool kick off the festive period with goals a-plenty at West Bromwich Albion, who are swept aside in a resounding 5-0 victory for Gerard Houllier's team. John Arne Riise opened the scoring after 18 minutes, before Florent Sinama-Pongolle and Steven Gerrard added a quick-fire double early in the second half. Riise scored the fourth with seven minutes to go before Spanish midfielder Luis Garcia completed the rout with just one minute of normal time remaining.

MONDAY 27th DECEMBER 1982

Kenny Dalglish scores a hat-trick as 44,664 watch Liverpool thrash Manchester City 5-2 at Anfield. Phil Neal and Ian Rush were also on target as Bob Paisley's team run wild against John Bond's side who would eventually be relegated at the end of the campaign, while Liverpool would go on to claim their 14th Division One title, their sixth under Paisley.

THURSDAY 28th DECEMBER 1893

Five different goalscorers are on target as Liverpool beat Crewe Alexandra 5-0 at Nantwich Road in a Second Division clash. Thomas Broadshaw – the first Liverpool player to receive an international call-up when he represented England against Ireland in February 1897 – scored along with Patrick Gordon, David Henderson, Hugh McQueen and former Third Lanark midfielder Malcolm McVean, who scored the club's first-ever Football League goal against Middlesbrough on September 2nd 1893.

SATURDAY 28th DECEMBER 1985

Kevin MacDonald scores as Liverpool hold Brian Clough's Nottingham Forest to a 1-1 draw. The result leaves the Reds three points adrift of leaders Manchester United in fourth position, though Liverpool will be crowned league champions just five months later.

SATURDAY 29th DECEMBER 1984

Kevin MacDonald makes his debut following his £400,000 move from Leicester City. The Scotsman, who started his career at Inverness Caledonian Thistle, made his first appearance at Anfield as Liverpool beat Luton Town 1-0 in a Division One fixture, with John Wark scoring the only goal. MacDonald made 65 appearances for the club, scoring just five times – all in the 1985/86 campaign – but just once in the league.

SATURDAY 30th DECEMBER 1995

Steve McManaman equalises twice for Liverpool in a 2-2 draw with Chelsea at Stamford Bridge. John Spencer had twice given the hosts an advantage in the Premier League clash in the capital, but academy graduate McManaman scored in either half to give Roy Evans' side a share of the spoils. The two sides had met before on this date in 1922, where they played out a 0-0 draw at Stamford Bridge.

SATURDAY 31st DECEMBER 1938

Liverpool end the year on a high note as Preston North End are comfortably beaten at Anfield. Two goals in as many minutes from Phil Taylor, and a penalty from Willie Fagan, put Liverpool in command before Jack Balmer added a third with five minutes to go. Taylor netted his second just three minutes later to round off a resounding 4-1 victory over Preston, leaving manager George Kay a happy man entering the New Year.

SATURDAY 31st DECEMBER 1977

Phil Thompson and Kenny Dalglish score second-half goals to give Liverpool a 2-0 win away to Newcastle United. The result is no surprise, with the Magpies sitting just one point off the bottom, while Bob Paisley's side are still six points behind leaders Nottingham Forest. The Reds will eventually finish runners-up in Division One.

SATURDAY 31st DECEMBER 1983

Ian Rush's first-half goal is enough to give Liverpool a 1-0 win away to Nottingham Forest. It's Forest's second home defeat of the season and it keeps the Reds three points clear of Manchester United.

KENNY DALGLISH – LFC ICON (SEE 31ST DECEMBER 1977).

SUNDAY 31st DECEMBER 2005

Peter Crouch's winning goal on 52 minutes is enough to give Liverpool a 1-0 win over West Bromwich Albion at Anfield. It still leaves the Reds 15 points adrift of leaders Chelsea, but with two games in hand.